Redwork

with a TWIST

10 fresh projects
by Pat Sloan

LEISURE ARTS, INC.
Little Rock, Arkansas

EDITORIAL STAFF
Editor-in-Chief: Susan White Sullivan
Quilt Publications Director: Cheryl Johnson
Special Projects Director:
  Susan Frantz Wiles
Senior Prepress Director: Mark Hawkins
Art Publications Director: Rhonda Shelby
Technical Editor: Lisa Lancaster
Technical Writer: Frances Huddleston
Editorial Writer: Susan McManus Johnson
Art Category Manager: Lora Puls
Graphic Designer: Amy Temple
Graphic Artists: Jacob Casleton and
  Janie Wright
Imaging Technician: Stephanie Johnson
Photography Director: Katherine Laughlin
Contributing Photostylist: Christy Myers
Contributing Photographer: Mark Matthews
Publishing Systems Administrator:
  Becky Riddle
Mac Information Technology Specialist:
  Robert Young

BUSINESS STAFF
President and Chief Executive Officer:
  Rick Barton
**Vice President and Chief Operations
  Officer:** Tom Siebenmorgen
Vice President of Sales: Mike Behar
Director of Finance and Administration:
  Laticia Mull Dittrich
National Sales Director: Martha Adams
Creative Services: Chaska Lucas
Information Technology Director:
  Hermine Linz
Controller: Francis Caple
Vice President, Operations: Jim Dittrich
Retail Customer Service Manager:
  Stan Raynor
Print Production Manager: Fred F. Pruss

Library of Congress Control Number:
2010933247 • ISBN-13: 978-1-60900-018-9

A note from Pat...

I do love the color red! Embroiderers in the late 1800s liked red, too, because that's when a colorfast dye called Turkey Red became available. Threads dyed with Turkey Red would never bleed or fade, which made redwork embroidery popular. After a while, "penny squares" were offered in catalogs and local variety stores. These fabric squares had a preprinted design for embroidery and were eventually put together into quilts.

I wanted to update this wonderful craft for quilters. My idea is still to embroider in only one color, but that color is your choice completely! The fabrics you use to finish your projects can be multi-colored prints just as easily as solids. My embroidery patterns are also new and fairly quick to stitch. So pick a pattern and get started—your redwork is calling!

—Pat

About Pat Sloan:
Quilters everywhere adore Pat Sloan's friendly approach to quilting, sewing, and needlecrafts. Learn more about Pat at PatSloan.com, and collect her books by visiting your local fabric store or LeisureArts.com.

Table of Contents

REDWORK
Supplies & Techniques

Thread

Six-strand embroidery floss or pearl cotton are commonly used for redwork, but there are many other choices. Here I've listed just a few suggestions. And of course, each of these come in many colors.

- **Six strand cotton embroidery floss.** You may use as many strands as you want, but I usually use 2 or 3 strands for most of my redwork. Project instructions specify how many strands I used.

- **Pearl Cotton.** Pearl cotton is a 2-ply, hi-sheen, twisted thread. DMC sizes #8 and #12 are good weights for redwork. Size #8 is the heavier of the two. Stitch using one thread.

- **Sulky® cotton thread.** This thread has a matte finish for a warm, natural look and feel. The 12 wt. works well for redwork. Stitch using one thread.

- **Aurifil™ Makò cotton thread.** Aurifil™ 12 wt. cotton thread is smooth and soft and produces excellent stitch definition. Stitch using one thread.

- **Aurifil™ Lana wool thread.** Aurifil™ wool thread is a textured thread made of 50% wool and 50% acrylic. It produces a soft appearance. The 12 wt. is a good choice for redwork and is thicker than many other embroidery threads. Stitch using one thread.

The type of thread that I used for the redwork on each project is included in the instructions for that project—but use another thread if you want. I suggest that you make a sample, trying various threads and various numbers of floss strands on a leftover piece of your fabric for redwork.

Fabric for Redwork

Since your redwork pieces will be part of a quilt or other pieced project, choose high-quality, medium-weight 100% cotton. If you prewash the other fabrics for your project, make sure you also prewash your fabric for redwork.

Redwork is traditionally worked on a solid or "almost solid" fabric, such as a cream tone-on-tone print, so that the fabric doesn't compete with the redwork. But you can use other fabrics. How about a red fabric with a cream thread or a hunter green fabric with a tan thread! Always do a test on a scrap piece of the fabric to make sure you love the look.

Needles

A needle with a sharp point is necessary to pierce the fabric and the eye needs to be large enough for the thread you choose. Embroidery, crewel, and chenille needles all have sharp points and large eyes. I like using embroidery needles, and for most threads, a 9 is a good size. If you want to try other needles, remember that the higher the number, the finer the needle.

Hoops

I don't use an embroidery hoop, but some people feel they can make nicer stitches while using one. A hoop will hold the fabric taut while you stitch and help keep you from pulling the thread too tight and puckering the fabric.

Hoops are available in many sizes and are made of wood or plastic. Embroiders often prefer one or the other, but both types will work just fine. You may want to use a small hoop for smaller pieces of redwork and a large hoop for larger pieces.

If you choose to use a hoop, be sure to loosen the hoop or remove your project at the end of each stitching session to prevent "hoop marks."

Other Tools

- **Needle threader.** There are many needle threaders on the market for thicker threads or multiple strands of floss.

- **Thimble.** A thimble is used to help push the needle through the fabric. It is worn on the middle finger of the stitching hand while embroidering. It may take a while to get used to wearing a thimble, but it will protect your fingertip.

- **Embroidery scissors.** Small, sharp embroidery scissors clip thread and floss quickly and neatly. Leather sheaths are available to protect the points of your scissors (and your fingers!).

Transferring the Design

My favorite way to transfer the design is to have a light source under the pattern and place the fabric on top.

Photocopy pattern page(s). Tape photocopy, right side up, on a light box or sunny window. Center your fabric, right side up, over the design (unless otherwise noted in project instructions) and tape in place. Trace the design directly onto the fabric using a sharp #2 pencil, chalk, or very fine permanent marker in your thread color.

Lining Your Fabric for Redwork

Because redwork (in any color) is often stitched on light fabric, thread ends "shadowing" to the front is often a problem. In the past, stitchers would weave the thread ends into the embroidery stitches on the back so no tails would show through to the front.

In more recent years, stitchers have started lining their fabric. Muslin is a good choice for lining. Or you can use a solid color 100% cotton fabric the same color as your fabric for redwork. The lining pieces should be cut the same sizes as the fabric pieces for redwork.

If you prewash the fabrics for your project, make sure you also prewash your lining. Press the fabric for redwork and lining together and then hand baste vertically and horizontally through the center and 1¹/₄" from the edges.

The Embroidery Stitches

The lines in the redwork designs can be stitched with Backstitches or Stem Stitches. Straight Stitches work well for short straight lines and French Knots can be added for small dots, such as eyes, strawberry seeds, and dots on the letters "i" and "j".

I begin and end my stitching with a simple single wrap knot to secure the "tails." To secure the tails of your thread without knots, and for a smoother back, begin by laying the thread flat against the back of the fabric and covering the tail with the first few stitches. Secure the other end of the thread by weaving it through a few stitches on the back and snipping off any left over length.

Backstitch

To work Backstitches, come up at 1, go down at 2, and come up at 3 (**Fig. 1**). Go down at 4 (same hole as 1). Coming up at 5, continue working in the same manner along traced line.

Fig. 1

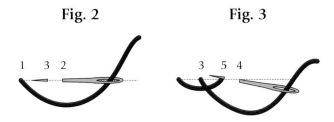

Stem Stitch

To work Stem Stitches, come up at 1. Keeping the thread *below* the needle, go down at 2, and come up at 3 (**Fig. 2**). Go down at 4 and come up at 5 (**Fig. 3**).

Fig. 2   **Fig. 3**

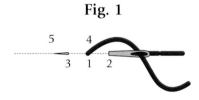

Straight Stitch

To work a Straight Stitch, come up at 1 and go down at 2 (**Fig. 4**).

Fig. 4

French Knot

Follow **Figs. 5–8** to complete French Knots. Come up at 1. Wrap thread once around needle and insert needle at 2, holding end of thread with non-stitching fingers. Tighten knot, then pull needle through, holding thread until it must be released.

Fig. 5   **Fig. 6**

Fig. 7   **Fig. 8**

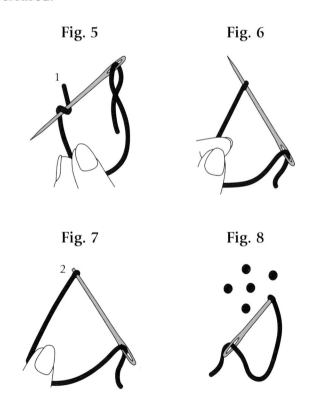

Around the T·O·W·N

Finished Quilt Size: 45³/₈" x 45³/₈" (115 cm x 115 cm)
Finished Block Size: 5⁵/₈" x 5⁵/₈" (14 cm x 14 cm)

Yardage Requirements

Yardage is based on 43"/44" (109 cm/112 cm) wide fabric.

- 1 yd (91 cm) of cream solid fabric for redwork
- 1 yd (91 cm) of fabric for redwork lining
- ¹/₈ yd (11 cm) *each* of yellow print #1 and yellow print #2 fabric for Blocks
- ¹/₄ yd (23 cm) of yellow print #3 fabric for sashings and 1st border
- ¹/₈ yd (11 cm) *each* of red print #1 and red print #2 fabric for Blocks
- ¹/₄ yd (23 cm) of red print #3 fabric for 3rd border
- ¹/₈ yd (11 cm) *each* of blue print #1 and blue print #2 fabric for Blocks
- 1³/₈ yds (1.3 m) of blue print #3 fabric for 4th border
- ¹/₄ yd (23 cm) of fabric for binding
- 3 yds (2.7 m) of fabric for backing

You will also need:

- 53" x 53" (135 cm x 135 cm) piece of batting
- Red pearl cotton #12

Cutting the Pieces

*Follow **Rotary Cutting**, page 88, to cut pieces. Cut all strips from the selvage-to-selvage width of the fabric unless otherwise indicated. Borders are cut exact length. Rectangles and large squares are cut larger than needed and will be trimmed after embroidering. All measurements include $^1/_4$" seam allowances.*

From cream solid fabric:
- Cut 4 strips $7^1/_2$"w. From these strips, cut 4 **rectangles** $7^1/_2$" x $22^7/_8$" and 4 **large squares** $7^1/_2$" x $7^1/_2$".

From fabric for redwork lining:
- Cut 4 strips $7^1/_2$"w. From these strips, cut 4 **rectangle linings** $7^1/_2$" x $22^7/_8$" and 4 **large square linings** $7^1/_2$" x $7^1/_2$".

From *each* of yellow print #1 and yellow print #2 fabric:
- Cut 1 strip 3"w. From this strip, cut 9 **small squares** 3" x 3".

From yellow print #3 fabric:
- Cut 2 strips $1^1/_2$"w. From these strips, cut 12 **sashings** $1^1/_2$" x $6^1/_8$".
- Cut 2 **side 1st borders** $1^1/_4$" x $20^7/_8$".
- Cut 2 **top/bottom 1st borders** $1^1/_4$" x $19^3/_8$".

From red print #1 fabric:
- Cut 1 strip 3"w. From this strip, cut 9 **small squares** 3" x 3".

  From remainder of strip,
  - Cut 1 strip $1^1/_2$"w. From this strip, cut 4 **sashing posts** $1^1/_2$" x $1^1/_2$".

From red print #2 fabric:
- Cut 1 strip 3"w. From this strip, cut 9 **small squares** 3" x 3".

From red print #3 fabric:
- Cut 2 **side 3rd borders** $1^1/_2$" x $30^7/_8$".
- Cut 2 **top/bottom 3rd borders** $1^1/_2$" x $32^7/_8$".

From *each* of blue print #1 and blue print #2 fabrics:
- Cut 1 strip $3^7/_8$"w. From this strip, cut 9 squares $3^7/_8$" x $3^7/_8$". Cut squares *once* diagonally to make 18 **triangles**.

From blue print #3 fabric:
- Cut 2 *lengthwise* **side 4th borders** $6^1/_2$" x $44^7/_8$".
- Cut 2 *lengthwise* **top/bottom 4th borders** $6^1/_2$" x $32^7/_8$".

From fabric for binding:
- Cut 5 **binding strips** $1^1/_2$"w.

Stitching the Redwork Pieces

Redwork patterns are on pages 11–19. Embroidery stitches are shown on page 5.

1. Refer to photo, page 7, and **Quilt Top Diagram**, page 10, and follow **Transferring the Design**, page 4, to transfer patterns onto the centers of **rectangles** and **large squares**.
2. Use **rectangle linings** and **large square linings** and refer to **Lining Your Fabric**, page 4, to line rectangles and large squares.
3. Using red pearl cotton, Backstitch designs.
4. Centering stitched designs, trim rectangles to $5^1/_2$" x $20^7/_8$" to make **2nd borders** and trim large squares to $5^1/_2$" x $5^1/_2$" to make **2nd border squares**.

Making the Blocks

*Follow **Machine Piecing**, page 89, and **Pressing**, page 90, to assemble quilt top. As you sew, measure your work to compare with the measurements provided, which include seam allowances, and adjust your seam allowance as needed.*

1. Draw a diagonal line (corner to corner) on wrong side of each yellow print #1 and yellow print #2 **small square**.

2. Matching right sides, place 1 yellow print #1 **small square** on top of 1 red print #1 **small square**. Stitch $1/4$" from each side of drawn line (**Fig. 1**). Cut along drawn line and press seam allowances to red fabric to make 2 **Triangle-Square A's**. Trim Triangle-Square A's to $2^1/2$" x $2^1/2$". Make 18 Triangle-Square A's.

Fig. 1

Triangle-Square A (make 18)

3. In the same manner, use yellow print #2 and red print #2 **small squares** to make 18 **Triangle-Square B's**. Trim Triangle-Square B's to $2^1/2$" x $2^1/2$".

Triangle-Square B (make 18)

4. Sew 1 **Triangle-Square A** and 1 **Triangle-Square B** together to make **Unit 1**. Make 18 Unit 1's.

Unit 1 (make 18)

5. Sew 2 **Unit 1's** together to make **Pinwheel**. Pinwheel should measure $4^1/2$" x $4^1/2$". Make 9 Pinwheels.

Pinwheel (make 9)

6. Matching center of long side of triangles to seams in Pinwheel, sew 2 blue print #1 **triangles** to opposite sides of 1 **Pinwheel** (**Fig. 2**).

Fig. 2

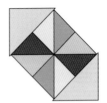

7. Sew 2 blue print #2 **triangles** to remaining sides of **Pinwheel** to make **Block**. Centering Pinwheel, trim **Block** to $6^1/8$" x $6^1/8$".
8. Repeat **Steps 6–7** to make 9 Blocks.

Block (make 9)

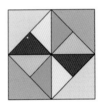

Assembling the Quilt Top Center

1. Sew 3 **Blocks** and 2 **sashings** together to make **Block Row**. Block Row should measure $19^3/8$" x $6^1/8$". Make 3 Block Rows.
2. Sew 3 **sashings** and 2 **sashing posts** together to make **Sashing Row**. Sashing Row should measure $19^3/8$" x $1^1/2$". Make 2 Sashing Rows.
3. Sew **Rows** together to make quilt top center. Quilt top center should measure $19^3/8$" x $19^3/8$".

Adding the Borders

1. Matching centers and corners, sew **top, bottom,** and then **side 1st borders** to quilt top center.
2. Matching centers and corners, sew **2nd borders** to top and bottom of quilt.
3. Sew one **2nd border square** to each end of remaining **2nd borders**. Matching centers and corners, sew 2nd borders to sides of quilt.
4. Matching centers and corners, sew **side,** and then **top** and **bottom 3rd borders** to quilt top.
5. Matching centers and corners, sew **top, bottom,** and then **side 4th borders** to quilt top. Quilt top should measure $44^7/8$" x $44^7/8$".

Completing the Quilt

1. Follow **Quilting**, page 91, to mark, layer, and quilt as desired. Quilt shown was machine quilted. The redwork motifs were outline quilted and swirls were quilted around the motifs. The sashings and narrow borders were outline quilted. Loops were quilted in the Pinwheels and a leaf and swirl pattern was quilted in the 4th border.

2. Follow **Making a Hanging Sleeve**, page 93, if a hanging sleeve is desired.

3. Use binding strips and follow **Making Single-Fold Straight-Grain Binding**, page 93, to make binding. Follow **Pat's Machine-Sewn Binding**, page 95, to bind quilt.

Quilt Top Diagram

Redwork patterns for
Around the Town
2nd border squares.

Redwork pattern for
Around the Town
top 2nd border.

*Join pattern, pages 12–13,
along grey dashed lines.*

Redwork pattern for
Around the Town
bottom 2nd border.

*Join pattern, pages 14–15,
along grey dashed lines.*

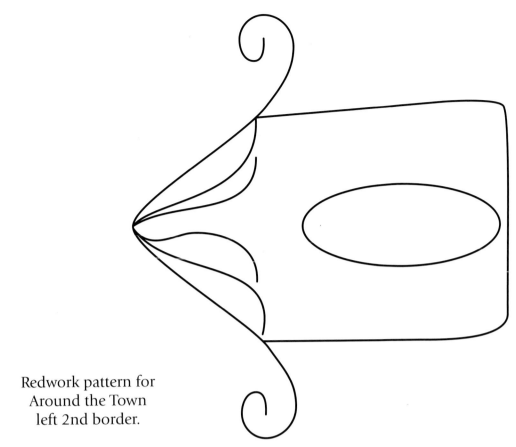

Redwork pattern for
Around the Town
left 2nd border.

*Join pattern, pages 16–17,
along grey dashed lines.*

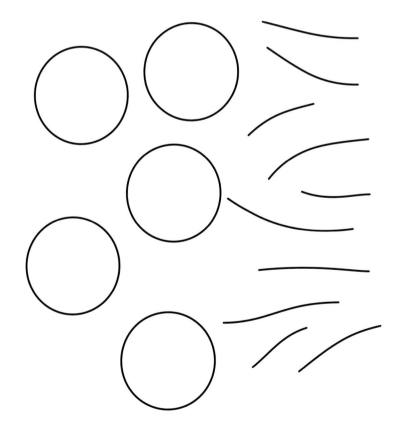

Redwork pattern for
Around the Town
right 2nd border.

*Join pattern, pages 18–19,
along grey dashed lines.*

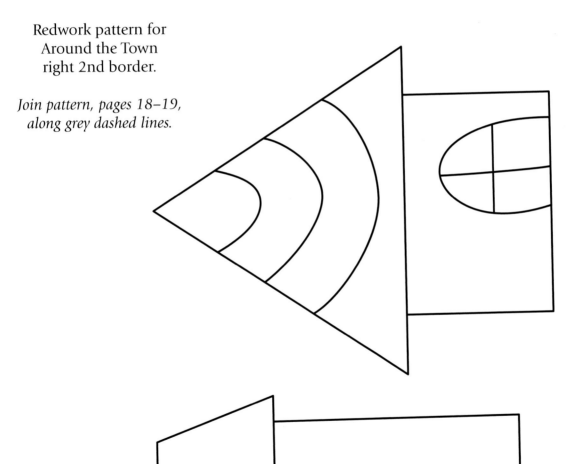

Around ᵗʰₑ Town
T·O·T·E

Finished Tote Size: 17¹/₂" x 12" x 4" (44 cm x 30 cm x 10 cm)

Yardage Requirements

Yardage is based on 43"/44" (109 cm/112 cm) wide fabric. Fat quarters are approximately 18" x 21" (46 cm x 53 cm). Fat eighths are approximately 9" x 21" (23 cm x 53 cm).

- ³/₈ yd (34 cm) *or* 1 fat quarter of white tone-on-tone print fabric for redwork
- ³/₈ yd (34 cm) *or* 1 fat quarter of fabric for redwork lining
- ¹/₂ yd (46 cm) of black/white floral print fabric for top and bottom of tote
- ¹/₈ yd (11 cm) *or* 1 fat eighth of white with small black print #1 fabric for sides of tote
- ³/₈ yd (34 cm) *or* 1 fat quarter of white with small black print #2 fabric for center back of tote
- ¹/₂ yd (46 cm) of black with tiny white dot print fabric for handles, binding, and trim
- ¹/₄ yd (23 cm) of white with small black dot print fabric for ruffle
- ⁷/₈ yd (80 cm) of white with large black dot fabric for tote lining

You will also need:
- 1³/₈ yds (1.3 m) of HeatnBond® fusible fleece (20" [51 cm] wide)
- Black pearl cotton #8

Cutting the Pieces

*Follow Rotary Cutting, page 88, to cut pieces.
Cut all strips from the selvage-to-selvage width
of the fabric unless otherwise noted. Redwork
rectangle is cut larger than needed and will be
trimmed after embroidering. All measurements
include $1/4$" seam allowances.*

From white tone-on-tone print fabric:
- Cut 1 **redwork rectangle** $18^1/2$" x $10^1/2$".

From lining fabric:
- Cut 1 **rectangle lining** $18^1/2$" x $10^1/2$".

From black/white floral print fabric:
- Cut 2 **top rectangles** 3" x 22".
- Cut 2 **bottom rectangles** $3^3/4$" x 22".

From white with small black print #1 fabric:
- Cut 4 **side rectangles** $3^1/4$" x $8^1/2$".

From white with small black print #2 fabric:
- Cut 1 **center back rectangle** $16^1/2$" x $8^1/2$".

From black with tiny white dot print fabric:
- Cut 2 **handles** $4^1/8$"w.
- Cut 2 **binding strips** $2^1/2$"w.
- Cut 2 **trim strips** $1^1/2$" x 22".

From white with small black dot print fabric:
- Cut 2 **ruffles** 3"w.

From white with large black dot print fabric:
- Cut 2 **front/back tote linings** 22" x $14^1/4$".

From fusible fleece:
- Cut 2 *lengthwise* **fleece strips** $1^1/2$" x the same length as the handles cut earlier (approximately 42").
- Cut 2 **fleece rectangles** 22" x $14^1/4$".

Stitching the Redwork Panel

Embroidery stitches are shown on page 5.

1. For redwork pattern, refer to photo, page 21, and select desired motifs from the Around the Town Quilt redwork patterns, pages 11–19. Entire design should be no larger than 15" x $6^1/4$".
2. Centering design horizontally 2" from bottom edge of rectangle, follow **Transferring the Design**, page 4, to transfer patterns onto **redwork rectangle**.
3. Use **rectangle lining** and refer to **Lining Your Fabric**, page 4, to line redwork rectangle.
4. Using black pearl cotton, Stem Stitch design.
5. With stitched design centered horizontally and leaving a 1" space below design, trim redwork rectangle to $16^1/2$" x $8^1/2$".

Making the Tote Front and Back

*Follow **Machine Piecing**, page 89, and **Pressing**, page 90, to assemble tote.*

1. Sew 2 **side rectangles** and **redwork rectangle** together to make **Unit 1**.

Unit 1

2. Sew **Unit 1**, 1 **top rectangle**, and 1 **bottom rectangle** together to make **tote front**.

Tote Front

3. Sew 2 **side rectangles** and **center back rectangle** together to make **Unit 2**.

Unit 2

4. Sew **Unit 2**, 1 **top rectangle**, and 1 **bottom rectangle** together to make **tote back**.

Tote Back

5. Following manufacturer's instructions, fuse **fleece rectangles** to wrong side of tote front and tote back.

Adding the Ruffles

1. Matching wrong sides and long edges, press each **ruffle** in half.
2. Stitch basting lines (longest stitch length) approximately $3/16$" and $1/8$" from long raw edges.
3. Using basting stitches, gather each ruffle to 22" long.
4. With long raw edge of ruffle aligned along seam below top rectangle, baste 1 ruffle to tote front $1/8$" from raw edges of ruffle. Repeat to baste ruffle to tote back.

Making the Handles

1. Press 1 long edge of 1 **handle** $1/4$" to the wrong side.
2. Fuse 1 **fleece strip** to wrong side of handle along unpressed long edge (**Fig. 1**).

Fig. 1

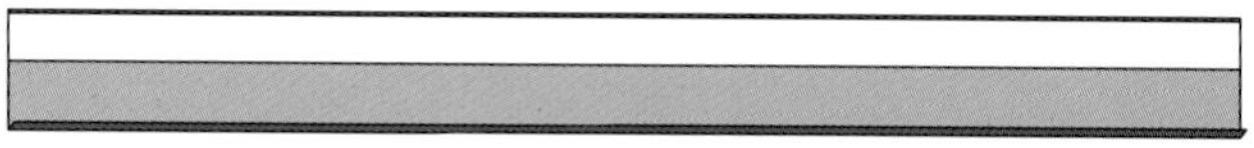

3. Fold unpressed edge along edge of fleece (**Fig. 2**), and then fold pressed edge along opposite edge of fleece (**Fig. 3**) so that handle measures $1^1/2$"w.

Fig. 2

Fig. 3

4. Referring to **Fig. 4**, topstitch along folded edge and each long edge of handle.

Fig. 4

5. Repeat **Steps 1–4** to make second handle.

Assembling the Tote

1. Press one long edge of each **trim strip** $1/4$" to wrong side.
2. Matching unpressed edge of trim strip and raw edge of ruffle, sew 1 trim strip to tote front $1/4$" from raw edges (**Fig. 5**).
3. With raw ends of 1 handle $1/8$" from unpressed edge of trim strip and 5" from sides of tote front, topstitch a rectangle near each end of handle as shown to attach handle.

Fig. 5

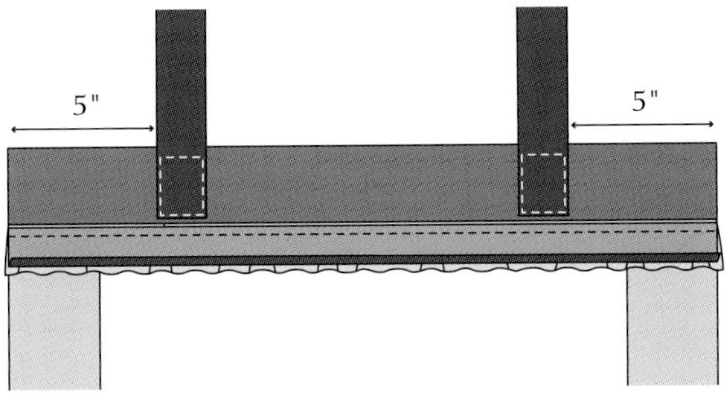

5"   5"

4. Fold and press trim strip over seam, covering raw edges of ruffle and handle. Topstitch along both long edges of trim strip.
5. Repeat **Steps 2–4** to sew handle and trim strip to tote back.
6. Matching right sides, sew tote front and tote back together along side and bottom edges.
7. For lining, match right sides and sew **lining front** and **lining back** together along side and bottom edges.

8. To box bottom of tote, match right sides and align tote side seam with bottom seam. Refer to **Fig. 6** to sew across corner 2" from tip. Repeat for remaining side and bottom seam. Turn tote right side out.

Fig. 6

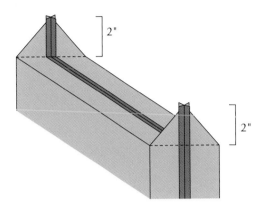

2"

2"

9. In the same manner, box bottom of lining. Do not turn lining right side out.
10. Matching **wrong** sides, place lining inside tote. Baste tote and lining together $1/8$" from top edge.
11. Use binding strips and follow **Making Double-Fold Straight-Grain Binding**, page 93, to make binding. Follow **Pat's Machine-Sewn Binding**, **Steps 2–3**, page 95, sewing binding to lining side of tote, folding binding to outside of tote, and Machine Blanket Stitching binding to outside of tote.

Liberty
B·L·U·E

Finished Quilt Size: 39" x 47" (99 cm x 119 cm)

Yardage Requirements

Yardage is based on 43"/44" (109 cm/112 cm) wide fabric.

1³/₄ yds (1.6 m) of cream tone-on-tone print fabric for redwork

1³/₈ yds (1.3 m) of fabric for redwork lining

³/₄ yd (69 cm) of cream floral print fabric

³/₈ yd (34 cm) of navy tone-on-tone print fabric

³/₄ yd (69 cm) of navy star print fabric

¹/₄ yd (23 cm) of fabric for binding

3¹/₈ yds (2.9 m) of fabric for backing

You will also need:

47" x 55" (119 cm x 140 cm) piece of batting

Navy Aurifil™ Makò 12 wt cotton thread

Cutting the Pieces

*Follow **Rotary Cutting**, page 88, to cut pieces. Cut all strips from the selvage-to-selvage width of the fabric. Pieces for redwork are cut larger than needed and will be trimmed after embroidering. All measurements include $1/4$" seam allowances.*

From cream tone-on-tone print fabric:
- Cut 1 strip $8^1/2$"w. From this strip, cut 4 **large squares** $8^1/2$" x $8^1/2$".
- Cut 4 strips 3"w. From these strips, cut 46 **medium squares** 3" x 3".
- Cut 2 **side 2nd borders** $4^1/2$" x $26^1/2$".
- Cut 2 **top/bottom 2nd borders** $4^1/2$" x $14^1/2$".
- Cut 1 **rectangle** $12^1/2$" x $20^1/2$".
- Cut 4 **small squares** $2^1/2$" x $2^1/2$".

From lining fabric:
- Cut 1 strip $8^1/2$"w. From this strip, cut 4 **large square linings** $8^1/2$" x $8^1/2$".
- Cut 2 **side 2nd border linings** $4^1/2$" x $26^1/2$".
- Cut 2 **top/bottom 2nd border linings** $4^1/2$" x $14^1/2$".
- Cut 1 **rectangle lining** $12^1/2$" x $20^1/2$".

From cream floral print fabric:
- Cut 4 **wide side border strips** 3" x $34^1/2$".
- Cut 4 **wide top/bottom border strips** 3" x $26^1/2$".

From navy tone-on-tone print fabric:
- Cut 4 strips 3"w. From these strips, cut 46 **medium squares** 3" x 3".

From navy star print fabric:
- Cut 2 strips 3"w. From these strips, cut 16 **medium squares** 3" x 3".
- Cut 2 **narrow side border strips** $1^1/2$" x $34^1/2$".
- Cut 2 **narrow top/bottom border strips** $1^1/2$" x $26^1/2$".
- Cut 2 **side 4th borders** $1^1/2$" x $32^1/2$".
- Cut 2 **top/bottom 4th borders** $1^1/2$" x $26^1/2$".
- Cut 2 **side 1st borders** $1^1/2$" x $20^1/2$".
- Cut 2 **top/bottom1st borders** $1^1/2$" x $10^1/2$".

From fabric for binding:
- Cut 5 **binding strips** $1^1/2$"w.

Stitching the Redwork Pieces

Redwork patterns are on pages 32–35. Embroidery stitches are shown on page 5.

1. Refer to photo, page 27, and **Quilt Top Diagram**, page 31, and follow **Transferring the Design**, page 4, to transfer patterns onto the centers of **rectangle**, **side**, **top**, and **bottom 2nd borders**, and **large squares**.
2. Use **rectangle lining**, **side**, **top**, and **bottom 2nd border linings**, and **large square linings** and refer to **Lining Your Fabric**, page 4, to line redwork pieces listed in **Step 1**.
3. Using navy Aurifil™ thread, Backstitch designs. Work French Knots for dots.
4. Centering stitched designs, trim redwork pieces as follows.
   - Rectangle: $10^1/2$" x $18^1/2$"
   - Side 2nd borders: $2^1/2$" x $24^1/2$"
   - Top/bottom 2nd borders: $2^1/2$" x $12^1/2$"
   - Large squares: $6^1/2$" x $6^1/2$"

Adding the 1st and 2nd Borders

*Follow **Machine Piecing**, page 89, and **Pressing**, page 90, to assemble quilt top. As you sew, measure your work to compare with the measurements provided, which include seam allowances, and adjust your seam allowance as needed.*

1. Sew **top**, **bottom**, and then **side 1st borders** to **rectangle**. Quilt top should now measure $12^{1}/_{2}$" x $20^{1}/_{2}$".

2. Sew **top**, **bottom**, and then **side 2nd borders** to quilt top. Quilt top should now measure $16^{1}/_{2}$" x $24^{1}/_{2}$".

Adding the 3rd Border

1. Draw a diagonal line (corner to corner) on wrong side of each cream **medium square**.

2. Matching right sides, place 1 cream **medium square** on top of 1 navy tone-on-tone **medium square**. Stitch $^{1}/_{4}$" from each side of drawn line (**Fig. 1**). Cut along drawn line and press seam allowances to navy fabric to make 2 **Triangle-Squares**. Trim Triangle-Squares to $2^{1}/_{2}$" x $2^{1}/_{2}$". Make 92 Triangle-Squares.

Fig. 1 **Triangle-Square** (make 92)

3. Sew 4 **Triangle-Squares** together to make **Unit 1**. Unit 1 should measure $4^{1}/_{2}$" x $4^{1}/_{2}$". Make 20 Unit 1's.

Unit 1 (make 20)

4. Sew 3 **Triangle-Squares** and 1 cream **small square** together to make **Unit 2**. Unit 2 should measure $4^{1}/_{2}$" x $4^{1}/_{2}$". Make 4 Unit 2's.

Unit 2 (make 4)

5. Sew 6 **Unit 1's** together to make **side 3rd border**. Side 3rd border should measure $4^{1}/_{2}$" x $24^{1}/_{2}$". Make 2 side 3rd borders.

Side 3rd Border (make 2)

6. Sew 4 **Unit 1's** and 2 **Unit 2's** together to make **top 3rd border**. Top 3rd border should measure $4^{1}/_{2}$" x $24^{1}/_{2}$". Repeat to make **bottom 3rd border**.

Top/Bottom 3rd Border (make 2)

7. Sew **side** and then **top** and **bottom 3rd borders** to quilt top. Quilt top should now measure $24^{1}/_{2}$" x $32^{1}/_{2}$".

Adding the 4th Border

1. Sew **side** and then **top** and **bottom** **4th borders** to quilt top. Quilt top should now measure 26^1/$_2$" x 34^1/$_2$".

Adding the 5th Border

1. With right sides together, place 1 navy star print **medium square** on 1 corner of 1 **large square** and stitch diagonally (**Fig. 2**). Trim ^{1}/$_4$" from stitching line (**Fig. 3**) and press open (**Fig. 4**).

Fig. 2	**Fig. 3**	**Fig. 4**

2. Continue adding navy **medium squares** to large square to make **border corner**. Border corner should measure 6^1/$_2$" x 6^1/$_2$". Make 4 border corners.

Border Corner (make 4)

3. Sew 2 **wide side border strips** and 1 **narrow side border strip** together to make **side 5th border**. Side 5th border should measure 6^1/$_2$" x 34^1/$_2$". Make 2 side 5th borders.

Side 5th Border (make 2)

4. Sew 2 **wide top/bottom border strips** and 1 **narrow top/bottom border strip** together to make **top 5th border**. Top 5th border should measure 6^1/$_2$" x 26^1/$_2$". Repeat to make **bottom 5th border**.

Top/Bottom 5th Border (make 2)

5. Sew 1 **border corner** to each end of top/bottom 5th borders.

6. Matching centers and corners, sew side and then top and bottom 5th borders to quilt top. Quilt top should measure 38^1/$_2$" x 46^1/$_2$".

Completing the Quilt

1. Follow **Quilting**, page 91, to mark, layer, and quilt as desired. Quilt shown was machine quilted. A leaf and vine pattern was quilted around the redwork with a loop quilted in each petal. The cream floral print strips of the 5th border were also quilted with a leaf and vine pattern. In the 3rd border, the navy zigzag pattern was outline quilted and swirls were quilted in the outer cream triangles. The navy star print 4th borders and strips in the 5th borders were quilted in the ditch.

2. Follow **Making a Hanging Sleeve**, page 93, if a hanging sleeve is desired.

3. Use binding strips and follow **Making Single-Fold Straight-Grain Binding**, page 93, to make binding. Follow **Pat's Machine-Sewn Binding**, page 95, to bind quilt.

Quilt Top Diagram

Redwork pattern for
Liberty Blue rectangle.

*Join pattern, pages 32–34,
along grey dashed lines.*

Redwork pattern for
Liberty Blue rectangle
(continued).

Redwork pattern for
Liberty Blue
top/bottom 2nd borders.

*Join pattern, pages 34–35,
along grey dashed lines.*

Redwork pattern for
Liberty Blue
border corners.

Redwork pattern for
Liberty Blue
side 2nd borders.

*Join pattern
along grey dashed lines.*

F·O·U·R
Seasons

Finished Quilt Size: 44" x 52" (112 cm x 132 cm)
Finished Block Size: 10" x 14" (25 cm x 36 cm)

Yardage Requirements

Yardage is based on 43"/44" (109 cm/112 cm) wide fabric.
$^7/_8$ yd (80 cm) of white tone-on-tone fabric for
  redwork
$^7/_8$ yd (80 cm) of fabric for redwork lining
$^5/_8$ yd (57 cm) *total* of assorted red print fabrics
$^5/_8$ yd (57 cm) *total* of assorted white print fabrics
$1^1/_8$ yds (1 m) of red toile fabric
$^3/_8$ yd (34 cm) of fabric for binding
$3^3/_8$ yds (3.1 m) of fabric for backing
You will also need:
  52" x 60" (132 cm x 152 cm) piece of batting
  Red 6 strand cotton embroidery floss

Cutting the Pieces

Follow Rotary Cutting, page 88, to cut pieces. Cut all strips from the selvage-to-selvage width of the fabric. Borders are cut exact length. Rectangles for redwork are cut larger than needed and will be trimmed after embroidering. All measurements include $^1/_4$" seam allowances.

From white tone-on-tone print fabric:
- Cut 4 **rectangles** $12^1/_2$" x $16^1/_2$".

From lining fabric:
- Cut 4 **rectangle linings** $12^1/_2$" x $16^1/_2$".

From assorted red print fabrics:
- Cut 21 **strips** $1^1/_2$" x 20".
- Cut 4 **squares** $1^1/_2$" x $1^1/_2$".

From assorted white print fabrics:
- Cut 21 **strips** $1^1/_2$" x 20".
- Cut 4 **squares** $1^1/_2$" x $1^1/_2$".
- Cut 1 **center square** $3^1/_2$" x $3^1/_2$".

From red toile print fabric:
- Cut 2 **side 4th borders** $6^1/_2$" x $39^1/_2$".
- Cut 2 **top/bottom 4th borders** $6^1/_2$" x $31^1/_2$".
- Cut 2 **side 2nd borders** $2^1/_2$" x $33^1/_2$".
- Cut 2 **top/bottom 2nd borders** $2^1/_2$" x $29/_2$".

From fabric for binding:
- Cut 6 **binding strips** $1^1/_2$"w.

Stitching the Redwork Blocks

Redwork patterns are on pages 42–49. Embroidery stitches are shown on page 5.

1. Refer to photo, page 37, and **Quilt Top Diagram**, page 41, and follow **Transferring the Design**, page 4, to transfer patterns onto the centers of **rectangles**.
2. Use **rectangle linings** and refer to **Lining Your Fabric**, page 4, to line rectangles.
3. Using 3 strands of red embroidery floss, Backstitch designs. Work French Knots for dots.
4. Centering stitched designs, trim rectangles to $10^1/_2$" x $14^1/_2$" to make **Blocks**.

Making the Checkerboard Units

*Follow **Machine Piecing**, page 89, and **Pressing**, page 90, to assemble quilt top. As you sew, measure your work to compare with the measurements provided, which include seam allowances, and adjust your seam allowance as needed.*

1. Sew 2 white **strips** and 1 red **strip** together to make **Strip Set A**. Strip Set A should measure 20" x $3^1/_2$". Make 2 Strip Set A's. Cut across Strip Set A's at $1^1/_2$" intervals to make 24 **Unit 1's**. Unit 1 should measure $1^1/_2$" x $3^1/_2$".

Strip Set A
(make 2)

Unit 1
(make 24)

$1^1/_2$"

2. Sew 2 red **strips** and 1 white **strip** together to make **Strip Set B**. Strip Set B should measure 20" x 3½". Make 2 Strip Set B's. Cut across Strip Set B's at 1½" intervals to make 24 **Unit 2's**. Unit 2 should measure 1½" x 3½".

Strip Set B
(make 2)

Unit 2
(make 24)

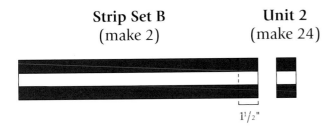

1½"

3. Sew 3 white **strips** and 3 red **strips** together to make **Strip Set C**. Strip Set C should measure 20" x 6½". Make 5 Strip Set C's. Cut across Strip Set C's at 1½" intervals to make 64 **Unit 3's**. Unit 3 should measure 1½" x 6½".

Strip Set C
(make 5)

Unit 3
(make 64)

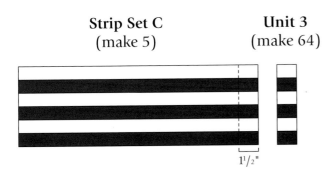

1½"

4. Sew 5 **Unit 1's** and 5 **Unit 2's** together to make **Unit 4**. Unit 4 should measure 10½" x 3½". Make 2 Unit 4's.

Unit 4 (make 2)

5. Sew 7 **Unit 1's** and 7 **Unit 2's** together to make **Unit 5**. Unit 5 should measure 14½" x 3½". Make 2 Unit 5's.

Unit 5 (make 2)

6. Sew 6 **Unit 3's** together to make **Unit 6**. Unit 6 should measure 6½" x 6½". Make 4 Unit 6's. Set aside remaining Unit 3's.

Unit 6 (make 4)

Assembling the Quilt Top Center

1. Sew **Spring Block**, 1 **Unit 5**, and **Summer Block** together to make **Top Row**. Top Row should measure 23½" x 14½".
2. Sew 2 **Unit 4's** and **center square** together to make **Middle Row**. Middle Row should measure 23½" x 3½".
3. Sew **Fall Block**, 1 **Unit 5**, and **Winter Block** together to make **Bottom Row**. Bottom Row should measure 23½" x 14½".
4. Sew **Rows** together to make quilt top center. Quilt top center should measure 23½" x 31½".

Adding the Borders

1. Sew 5 **Unit 3's** and 1 red **square** together to make **side 1st border**. Side 1st border should measure $1^1/_2$" x $31^1/_2$". Make 2 side 1st borders. Matching centers and corners, sew side 1st borders to quilt top center.

2. Sew 4 **Unit 3's** and 1 white **square** together to make **top 1st border**. Top 1st border should measure $1^1/_2$" x $25^1/_2$". Repeat to make **bottom 1st border**. Matching centers and corners, sew top/bottom 1st borders to quilt top center. Quilt top should now measure $25^1/_2$" x $33^1/_2$".

3. Matching centers and corners, sew **side** and then **top** and **bottom 2nd borders** to quilt top. Quilt top should now measure $29^1/_2$" x $37^1/_2$".

4. Sew 6 **Unit 3's** and 1 white **square** together to make **side 3rd border**. Side 3rd border should measure $1^1/_2$" x $37^1/_2$". Make 2 side 3rd borders. Matching centers and corners, sew side 3rd borders to quilt top.

5. Sew 5 **Unit 3's** and 1 red **square** together to make **top 3rd border**. Top 3rd border should measure $1^1/_2$" x $31^1/_2$". Repeat to make bottom 3rd border. Matching centers and corners, sew top/bottom 3rd borders to quilt top. Quilt top should now measure $31^1/_2$" x $39^1/_2$".

6. Matching centers and corners, sew **side 4th borders** to quilt top.

7. Sew 1 **Unit 6** to each end of **top/bottom 4th borders**. Matching center and corners, sew top/bottom 4th borders to quilt top. Quilt top should now measure $43^1/_2$" x $51^1/_2$".

Completing the Quilt

1. Follow **Quilting**, page 91, to mark, layer, and quilt as desired. Quilt shown was machine quilted. The checkerboards in the quilt top center and 1st and 3rd borders were diagonally crosshatch quilted. The checkerboards in the corners were quilted in the ditch and the 2nd and 4th borders were channel quilted.

2. Follow **Making a Hanging Sleeve**, page 93, if a hanging sleeve is desired.

3. Use binding strips and follow **Making Single-Fold Straight-Grain Binding**, page 93, to make binding. Follow **Pat's Machine-Sewn Binding**, page 95, to bind quilt.

Redwork pattern for Four Seasons Summer Block.

Join pattern, pages 42–43, along dashed grey lines.

Summer

Redwork pattern for
Four Seasons
Winter Block.

Join pattern, pages 44–45,
along dashed grey lines.

Redwork pattern for
Four Seasons
Fall Block.

*Join pattern, pages 46–47,
along dashed grey lines.*

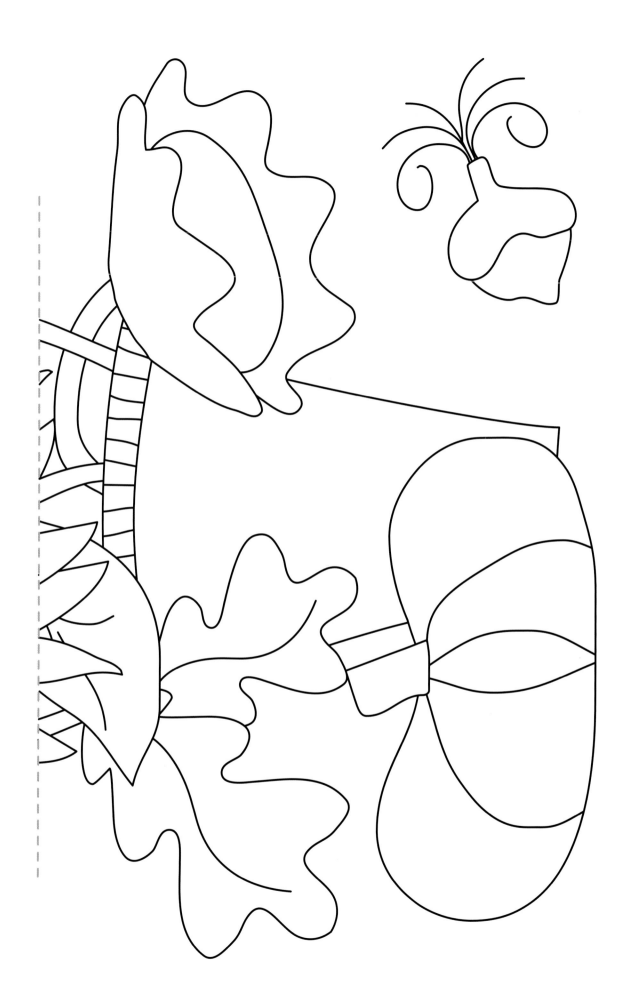

Redwork pattern for
Four Seasons
Spring Block.

*Join pattern, pages 48–49,
along dashed grey lines.*

SPRING

a Y·E·A·R in Stitches

Finished Quilt Size: 49" x 64" (124 cm x 163 cm)
Finished Block Size: 10" x 10" (25 cm x 25 cm)

Yardage Requirements

Yardage is based on 43"/44" (109 cm/112 cm) wide fabric.

- 1⁵/₈ yd (1.5 m) of pale yellow print fabric for redwork
- 1⁵/₈ yd (1.5 m) of fabric for redwork lining
- ³/₈ yd (34 cm) of cream print fabric
- ³/₄ yd (69 cm) of green print fabric
- 1¹/₂ yds (1.4 m) of burgundy large print fabric
- ¹/₂ yd (46 cm) of burgundy small print fabric
- ³/₈ yd (34 cm) of fabric for binding
- 4 yds (3.7 m) of fabric for backing

You will also need:

- 57" x 72" (145 cm x 183 cm) piece of batting
- Brown pearl cotton #8

Cutting the Pieces

Follow **Rotary Cutting**, *page 88, to cut pieces. Cut all strips from the selvage-to-selvage width of the fabric. Large squares for redwork are cut larger than needed and will be trimmed after embroidering. All measurements include $1/4$" seam allowances.*

From pale yellow print fabric:
- Cut 4 strips $12^1/2$"w. From these strips, cut 12 **large squares** $12^1/2$" x $12^1/2$".

From fabric for lining:
- Cut 4 strips $12^1/2$"w. From these strips, cut 12 **large square linings** $12^1/2$" x $12^1/2$".

From cream print fabric:
- Cut 6 strips $1^1/2$"w. From these strips, cut 17 **strips B** $1^1/2$" x 12".

From green print fabric:
- Cut 4 strips 4"w. From these strips, cut 33 **medium squares** 4" x 4" and 4 **small squares** $3^1/2$" x $3^1/2$".
- Cut 2 strips $2^1/2$"w. From these strips, cut 4 **strips C** $2^1/2$" x 20".
- Cut 1 **strip F** $1^1/2$" x 10".

From burgundy large print fabric:
- Cut 4 strips 4"w. From these strips, cut 33 **medium squares** 4" x 4".
- Cut 12 strips $2^1/2$"w. From these strips, cut 34 **strips A** $2^1/2$" x 12".

From burgundy small print fabric:
- Cut 1 strip $1^1/2$"w. From these strips, cut 2 **strips D** $1^1/2$" x 20".
- Cut 1 strip $2^1/2$"w. From this strip, cut 2 **strips E** $2^1/2$" x 10".
- Cut 6 **inner border strips** $1^1/2$"w.

From fabric for binding:
- Cut 7 **binding strips** $1^1/2$"w.

Stitching the Redwork Blocks

Redwork patterns are on pages 56–67. Embroidery stitches are shown on page 5.

1. Refer to photo, page 51, and **Quilt Top Diagram**, page 55, and follow **Transferring the Design**, page 4, to transfer patterns onto the centers of **large squares**.
2. Use **large square linings** and refer to **Lining Your Fabric**, page 4, to line large squares.
3. Using brown pearl cotton, Straight Stitch "X's" on flag in **Old Glory Block**, work French Knots for dots, and Stem Stitch everything else.
4. Centering stitched designs, trim large squares to $10^1/2$" x $10^1/2$" to make **Blocks**.

Making the Sashings and Sashing Posts

*Follow **Machine Piecing**, page 89, and **Pressing**, page 90, to assemble the quilt top. As you sew, measure your work to compare with the measurements provided, which include seam allowances, and adjust your seam allowance as needed.*

1. Sew 2 **strips A** and 1 **strip B** together to make **sashing**. Trim sashing to $10^1/2$" x $5^1/2$". Make 17 sashings.

Sashing (make 17)

2. Sew 2 **strips C** and 1 **strip D** together to make **Strip Set A**. Strip Set A should measure 20" x $5^1/_2$". Make 2 Strip Set A's. Cut across Strip Set A's at $2^1/_2$" intervals to make 12 **Unit 1's**. Unit 1 should measure $2^1/_2$" x $5^1/_2$".

Strip Set A (make 2)   **Unit 1** (make 12)

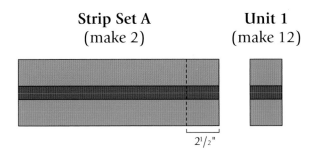

$2^1/_2$"

3. Sew 2 **strips E** and **strip F** together to make **Strip Set B**. Strip Set B should measure 10" x $5^1/_2$". Cut across Strip Set B at $1^1/_2$" intervals to make 6 **Unit 2's**. Unit 2 should measure $1^1/_2$" x $5^1/_2$".

Strip Set B   **Unit 2** (make 6)

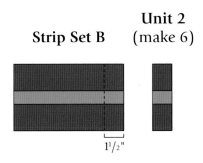

$1^1/_2$"

4. Sew 2 **Unit 1's** and 1 **Unit 2** together to make **sashing post**. Sashing post should measure $5^1/_2$" x $5^1/_2$". Make 6 sashing posts.

Sashing Post (make 6)

Assembling the Quilt Top Center

1. Sew 3 **Blocks** and 2 **sashings** together to make **Block Row**. Block Row should measure $40^1/_2$" x $10^1/_2$". Make 4 Block Rows.
2. Sew 3 **sashings** and 2 **sashing posts** together to make **Sashing Row**. Sashing Row should measure $40^1/_2$" x $5^1/_2$". Make 3 Sashing Rows.
3. Sew **Rows** together to make quilt top center. Quilt top center should measure $40^1/_2$" x $55^1/_2$".

Adding the Inner Border

1. Using diagonal seams (**Fig. 1**), sew **inner border strips** together into a continuous strip.

Fig. 1

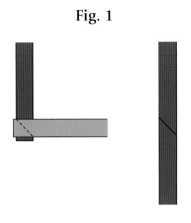

2. To determine length of **top/bottom inner borders**, measure *width* across center of quilt top center. Cut 2 top/bottom inner borders from continuous strip. Matching centers and corners, sew top/bottom inner borders to quilt top center.
3. To determine length of **side inner borders**, measure *length* across center of quilt top center (including added borders). Cut 2 side inner borders from continuous strip. Matching centers and corners, sew side inner borders to quilt top center. Quilt top should now measure $42^1/_2$" x $57^1/_2$".

Adding the Outer Border

1. Draw a diagonal line (corner to corner) on wrong side of each green **medium square**.
2. Matching right sides, place 1 green **medium square** on top of 1 burgundy **medium square**. Stitch ¹/₄" from each side of drawn line (**Fig. 2**). Cut along drawn line and press seam allowances to darker fabric to make 2 **Triangle-Squares**. Trim Triangle-Squares to 3¹/₂" x 3¹/₂". Make 66 Triangle-Squares.

Fig. 2

Triangle-Square (make 66)

3. Sew 19 **Triangle-Squares** together to make **left outer border**. Left outer border should measure 3¹/₂" x 57¹/₂".

Left Outer Border

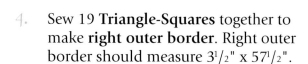

4. Sew 19 **Triangle-Squares** together to make **right outer border**. Right outer border should measure 3¹/₂" x 57¹/₂".

Right Outer Border

5. Matching centers and corners, sew left and right outer borders to quilt top.
6. Sew 14 **Triangle-Squares** and 2 green **small squares** together to make **top outer border**. Top outer border should measure 3¹/₂" x 48¹/₂".

Top Outer Border

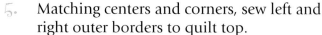

7. Sew 14 **Triangle-Squares** and 2 green **small squares** together to make **bottom outer border**. Bottom outer border should measure 3¹/₂" x 48¹/₂".

Bottom Outer Border

8. Matching centers and corners, sew **top** and **bottom outer borders** to quilt top. Quilt top should measure 48¹/₂" x 63¹/₂".

Completing the Quilt

1. Follow **Quilting**, page 91, to mark, layer, and quilt as desired. Quilt shown was machine quilted. The redwork designs were outline quilted. The areas around the redwork in the Blocks and green portions of the outer border were meander quilted. Large X's were quilted in each sashing post. A squiggly line through the center and straight lines near the edges were quilted in each burgundy strip in the sashings. The inner border and burgundy triangles were outline quilted with large loops in the triangles.
2. Follow **Making a Hanging Sleeve**, page 93, if a hanging sleeve is desired.
3. Use binding strips and follow **Making Single-Fold Straight-Grain Binding**, page 93, to make binding. Follow **Pat's Machine-Sewn Binding**, page 95, to bind quilt.

Add a Cherry on Top

OLD GLORY

By The Sea You Forget to Count The Days

SUNFLOWERS

a Y·E·A·R in Stitches
PILLOW & SLEEVES

Finished Pillow Size: 20" x 20" (51 cm x 51 cm)
Finished Pillow Sleeve Size: 13^1/$_2$" x 20" (34 cm x 51 cm)

Yardage Requirements

Yardage is based on 43"/44" (109 cm/112 cm) wide fabric. Instructions are for 1 pillow and 1 pillow sleeve.

For Pillow:
  1^3/$_8$ yds (1.3 m) of fabric
You will also need:
  20" x 20" (51 cm x 51 cm) pillow form

> **Tip:** *Choose a fabric with many colors for your pillow so that you will have lots of coordinating fabric choices for your sleeves. Or choose a solid neutral for your pillow, and switch out colorful sleeves every month of the year!*

For Pillow Sleeve:
  ^{3}/$_8$ yd (34 cm) of cream solid or tone-on-tone print fabric for redwork
  ^{3}/$_8$ yd (34 cm) of fabric for redwork lining
  ^{3}/$_4$ yd (69 cm) of print fabric for sleeve front and back
  ^{1}/$_4$ yd (23 cm) of fabric for binding
  1^1/$_4$ yds (1.1 m) of muslin for sleeve lining
You will also need:
  Embroidery floss or thread for redwork
  Optional: Embellishments such as buttons, rickrack, beads, or charms

Cutting the Pieces

*Follow **Rotary Cutting**, page 88, to cut pieces. Cut all strips from the selvage-to-selvage width of the fabric unless otherwise noted. Rectangle for redwork is cut larger than needed and will be trimmed after embroidering. Pillow front and back measurements include $1/2$" seam allowances. All other measurements include $1/4$" seam allowances.*

For Pillow:

From fabric:
- Cut 1 **pillow front** 21" x 21".
- Cut 2 **pillow back rectangles** 13" x 21".

For Pillow Sleeve:

From cream solid or tone-on-tone print fabric:
- Cut 1 **rectangle** $10^{1}/2$" x $14^{1}/2$".

From fabric for lining:
- Cut 1 **rectangle lining** $10^{1}/2$" x $14^{1}/2$".

From print fabric:
- Cut 2 *lengthwise* **side borders** 3" x $20^{1}/2$".
- Cut 2 **top/bottom borders** $8^{1}/2$" x $4^{1}/2$".
- Cut 1 **sleeve back** $13^{1}/2$" x $20^{1}/2$".

From fabric for binding:
- Cut 3 **binding strips** $2^{1}/4$"w.

From muslin:
- Cut 1 **sleeve lining** $13^{1}/2$" x $40^{1}/2$".

Making The Pillow

1. On each **pillow back rectangle**, press 1 long edge $1/4$" to wrong side; press $1/4$" to wrong side again and stitch in place.
2. Overlap hemmed edges of pillow back rectangles, right sides facing up, to form a 21" x 21" square. Baste pillow back rectangles together at overlap.
3. With right sides facing, pin **pillow front** and pillow back together. Sew around pillow using a $1/2$" seam allowance. Remove basting, turn, and press. Insert pillow form.

Stitching the Redwork Rectangle

Redwork patterns are on pages 56–67. Embroidery stitches are shown on page 5.

1. Refer to photo, page 51, and **Quilt Top Diagram** for the Year in Stitches quilt, page 55, to choose one redwork design. Follow **Transferring the Design**, page 4, to transfer pattern onto the center of **rectangle**.
2. Use **rectangle lining** and refer to **Lining Your Fabric**, page 4, to line rectangle.
3. Using floss or thread, stitch design as desired.
4. Centering stitched design, trim rectangle to $8^{1}/2$" x $12^{1}/2$".

Making the Sleeve Front

*Follow **Machine Piecing**, page 89, and **Pressing**, page 90, to make sleeve. Use ¹/₄" seam allowances throughout.*

1. Sew **top**, **bottom**, and then **side borders** to **rectangle** to make **sleeve front**. Sleeve front should measure 13¹/₂" x 20¹/₂".

Sleeve Front

2. With right sides together, sew sleeve front and sleeve back together along top and bottom edges to form sleeve. Turn sleeve right side out.

3. Matching right sides, sew short edges of **sleeve lining** together. Do not turn lining right side out.

4. With **wrong** sides together, place sleeve lining inside sleeve. Baste layers together along raw edges.

5. Use binding strips and follow **Making Double-Fold Straight-Grain Binding**, page 93, to make binding. Follow **Attaching Binding**, **Steps 1** and **6–15**, page 93, to bind raw edges of sleeve.

6. Add embellishments to sleeve front if desired.

Notions
K·E·E·P·E·R

Finished Keeper Size: 10" x 10" (25 cm x 25 cm)

Yardage Requirements

Yardage is based on 43"/44" (109 cm/112 cm) wide fabric.

³/₈ yd (34 cm) of muslin fabric for redwork and redwork lining

³/₈ yd (34 cm) of red print #1 fabric for back, spine, strip on front, small pocket, large pocket flap, and pincushion

³/₈ yd (34 cm) of red print #2 fabric for inner keeper

¹/₄ yd (23 cm) of red print #3 fabric for strip on front and binding

Scraps of assorted red print fabrics for 3 strips on front

³/₈ yd (34 cm) of black print fabric for large pocket, small pocket flap, scissor pocket, and strips on front

You will also need:

1³/₈ yds (1.3 m) of HeatnBond® fusible fleece (20" [51 cm] wide)

12" (30 cm) length of ³/₄" (19 mm) wide black hook and loop fastener

Red pearl cotton #8

2 black buttons, approximately 1" (25 mm) diameter each

1 yd (91 cm) of black ³/₁₆" (5 mm) wide ribbon

Cutting the Pieces

*Follow **Rotary Cutting**, page 88, to cut pieces. Cut all strips from the selvage-to-selvage width of the fabric. Muslin square and rectangle for redwork are cut larger than needed and will be trimmed after embroidering. All measurements include ¹/₄" seam allowances.*

From muslin fabric:
- Cut 1 **redwork square** $8^1/_2$" x $8^1/_2$".
- Cut 1 **redwork rectangle** $5^1/_2$" x 5".
- Cut 1 **square lining** $8^1/_2$" x $8^1/_2$".
- Cut 1 **rectangle lining** $5^1/_2$" x 5".

From red print #1 fabric:
- Cut 1 **square** $10^1/_2$" x $10^1/_2$".
- Cut 2 **large rectangles** 2" x $10^1/_2$".
- Cut 2 **small pockets** $5^1/_2$" x $5^1/_2$".
- Cut 2 **large pocket flaps** 9" x $2^1/_2$".
- Cut 1 **strip #3** $1^1/_2$" x $7^1/_2$".
- Cut 1 **strip #8** $1^1/_2$" x $10^1/_2$".
- Cut 2 **small rectangles** $2^1/_4$" x 3".
- Cut 1 **medium rectangle** 7" x 3".

From red print #2 fabric:
- Cut 2 **squares** $10^1/_2$" x $10^1/_2$".

From red print #3 fabric:
- Cut 2 **binding strips** $2^1/_4$"w.
- Cut 1 **strip #4** $1^1/_2$" x $8^1/_2$".

From scraps of red print fabrics:
- Cut 1 **strip #2** $1^1/_2$" x $7^1/_2$".
- Cut 1 **strip #5** $1^1/_2$" x $8^1/_2$".
- Cut 1 **strip #7** $1^1/_2$" x $9^1/_2$".

From black print fabric:
- Cut 2 **large pockets** $8^1/_2$" x 8".
- Cut 1 **strip #1** $1^1/_2$" x $6^1/_2$".
- Cut 1 **strip #6** $1^1/_2$" x $9^1/_2$".
- Cut 2 **small pocket flaps** 6" x $2^1/_2$".
- Cut 2 **scissor pockets** from pattern on page 77.

From fusible fleece:
- Cut 2 **large fleece rectangles** 22" x $10^1/_2$".
- Cut 1 **small fleece rectangle** $2^1/_2$" x $6^1/_2$".

Stitching the Redwork Pieces

Redwork patterns are on page 77. Embroidery stitches are shown on page 5.

1. Refer to photo, page 73, and follow **Transferring the Design**, page 4, to transfer patterns onto the centers of **redwork square** and **redwork rectangle**.
2. Use **square lining** and **rectangle lining** and refer to **Lining Your Fabric**, page 4, to line redwork square and redwork rectangle.
3. Using red pearl cotton, Backstitch designs.
4. Centering stitched designs, trim redwork square to $6^1/_2$" x $6^1/_2$" and redwork rectangle to $3^1/_2$" x 3".

Redwork Square

Redwork Rectangle

Making the Outer Keeper

*Follow **Machine Piecing**, page 89, and **Pressing**, page 90, to make outer keeper. Use ¹/₄" seam allowances throughout.*

1. Sew **Strip #1**, then **Strip #2** to **redwork square** to make **Unit 1**.

Unit 1

2. Sew **Strip #3**, then **Strip #4** to **Unit 1** to make **Unit 2**.

Unit 2

3. Sew **Strip #5**, then **Strip #6** to **Unit 2** to make **Unit 3**.

Unit 3

4. Sew **Strip #7**, then **Strip #8** to **Unit 3** to make **Block**. Block should measure $10^1/2$" x $10^1/2$".

Block

5. Sew **Block**, red print #1 **square**, and 1 **large rectangle** together to make outer keeper. Outer keeper should measure 22" x $10^1/2$".

Outer Keeper

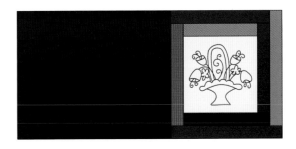

6. Following manufacturer's instructions, fuse 1 **large fleece rectangle** to wrong side of outer keeper.

Making the Inner Keeper

1. Matching right sides and leaving an opening for turning, sew 2 **large pockets** together. Turn large pocket right side out and stitch opening closed.
2. Cut a 7" length of hook and loop fastener strip. Centering strip horizontally, sew loop side of strip $1/4$" from 1 edge (top) of large pocket. Centering strip horizontally on right side of flap, sew hook side of strip $1/2$" from 1 long (bottom) edge of 1 **large pocket flap**.
3. Matching right sides and leaving an opening for turning, sew 2 **large pocket flaps** together. Turn large pocket flap right side out and stitch opening closed. Topstitch along side and bottom edges of large flap.
4. Repeat Steps 1–3 using **small pockets** and **small pocket flaps** and cutting a 4" length of hook and loop fastener strip.
5. Matching right sides and leaving an opening for turning, sew 2 **scissor pockets** together. Turn scissor pocket right side out and stitch opening closed.

6. Sew **redwork rectangle** and 2 **small rectangles** together to make **Unit 4**. Center and fuse **small fleece rectangle** to wrong side of Unit 4.

Unit 4

7. Matching right sides and leaving an opening for turning, sew **Unit 4** and **medium rectangle** together to make **pincushion**. Turn pincushion right side out and stitch opening closed.

8. Sew 2 red print #2 **squares** and 1 **large rectangle** together to make **Unit 5**. Unit 5 should measure 22" x 10½".

Unit 5

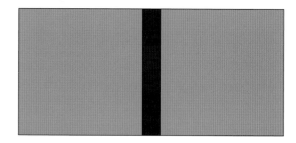

9. Fuse 1 **large fusible rectangle** to wrong side of Unit 5.

10. Arrange pockets and pincushion on Unit 5 as shown in **Inner Keeper** diagram; pin in place.

11. Follow **Machine Blanket Stitch**, page 90, to blanket stitch all edges of pincushion to Unit 5. Blanket stitch side and bottom edges of pockets to Unit 5. Fasten hook and loop strips on pockets and pocket flaps. Blanket stitch top edges of pocket flaps to Unit 5.

12. Sew 1 button to large pocket flap. For scissor ribbon, tack 1 end of ribbon above scissor pocket and then sew 1 button on top of ribbon end. Fold and place ribbon inside scissor pocket to keep it out of the way until keeper is completed.

Completing the Keeper

1. Layer outer keeper, right side down, and inner keeper, right side up. Pin baste layers together. Topstitch through center of large rectangle from top edge to bottom edge.

2. Use binding strips and follow **Making Double-Fold Straight-Grain Binding**, page 93, to make binding. Follow **Attaching Binding**, page 93, to bind keeper.

3. Tie ribbon end to scissors and insert scissors into scissor pocket.

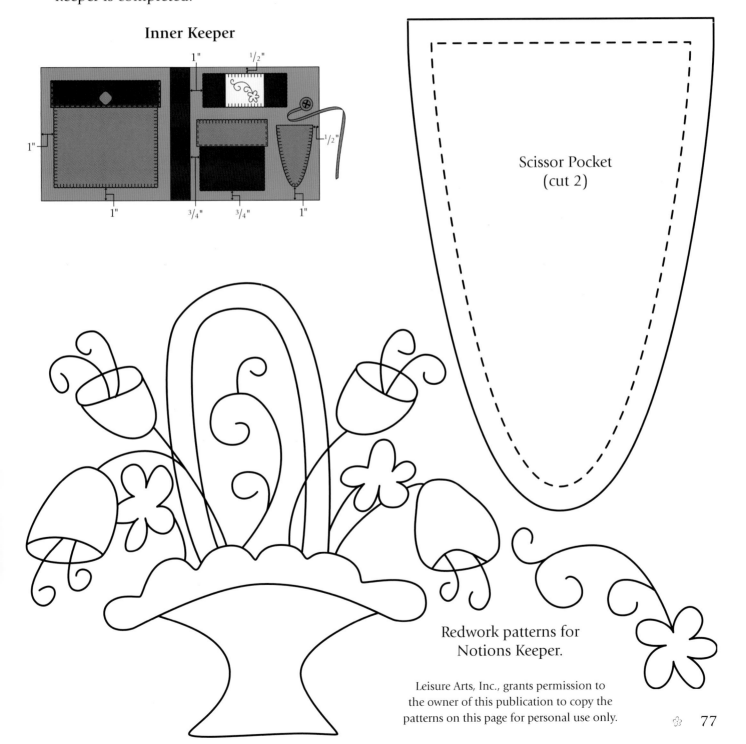

Inner Keeper

1"   1/2"

1"

1"   3/4"   3/4"   1"

1/2"

Scissor Pocket (cut 2)

Redwork patterns for Notions Keeper.

Finished Keeper Size: 5" x 4" x 6"
(13 cm x 10 cm x 15 cm)

Yardage Requirements

*Yardage is based on 43"/44"
(109 cm/112 cm) wide fabric.*
- ¼ yd (23 cm) of muslin fabric for redwork and redwork lining
- ⅜ yd (34 cm) of black print fabric
- 4" x 13" (10 cm x 33 cm) piece of red print fabric

You will also need:
- Red pearl cotton #8
- ⅜ yd (34 cm) of HeatnBond® fusible fleece (20" [51 cm] wide)

Cutting the Pieces

*Follow **Rotary Cutting**, page 88, to cut pieces. Rectangles for redwork are cut larger than needed and will be trimmed after embroidering. All measurements include ¼" seam allowances.*

From muslin fabric:
- Cut 2 **redwork rectangles** 5½" x 5".
- Cut 2 **rectangle linings** 5½" x 5".

From black print fabric:
- Cut 1 **large rectangle** 9½" x 11".
- Cut 1 **thread catcher lining** 9½" x 16½".

From red print fabric:
- Cut 4 **small rectangles** 3½" x 3".

From fusible fleece:
- Cut 1 **fleece rectangle** 9½" x 16".

·THREAD· CATCHER

Stitching the Redwork Pieces

Use the strawberry pattern, page 14, from Around the Town quilt. Or you may choose to use another small design from any of the other projects that is smaller than 3" x 2½". Embroidery stitches are shown on page 5.

1. Refer to photo and follow **Transferring the Design**, page 4, to transfer strawberry pattern onto each **redwork rectangle**.
2. Use **lining rectangles** and refer to **Lining Your Fabric**, page 4, to line redwork rectangles.
3. Using red pearl cotton, Stem Stitch designs. Randomly place French Knots for seeds.
4. Centering stitched designs, trim redwork rectangles to 3½" x 3".

Making the Thread Catcher

*Follow **Machine Piecing**, page 89, and **Pressing**, page 90, to make thread catcher. Use $1/4$" seam allowances throughout.*

1. Sew 1 **redwork rectangle** and 2 **small rectangles** together to make **Unit 1**. Make 2 Unit 1's.

Unit 1 (make 2)

2. Sew 2 **Unit 1's** and **large rectangle** together to make **outer catcher**.

Outer Catcher

3. Following manufacturer's instructions, fuse **fleece rectangle** to wrong side of outer catcher.

4. Matching right sides and short edges, sew sides of outer catcher together.

5. To box bottom, match right sides and align catcher side seams with center of catcher bottom. Refer to **Fig. 1** to sew across point 2" from tip. Repeat for remaining side seam and bottom. Fold points toward bottom of catcher. Turn right side out.

Fig. 1

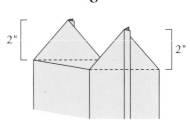

6. Matching right sides and short edges, sew sides of **thread catcher lining** together.

7. In the same manner as outer catcher, box bottom of lining. Press top edge $1/4$" to wrong side twice. Do not turn right side out.

8. Matching wrong sides and aligning side seams, place lining into outer catcher. Place folded top edge of lining over raw top edge of outer catcher. Follow **Machine Blanket Stitch**, page 90, to sew lining edge in place.

Finished Pincushion Size:
7" x 7" x 1¹/₂" (18 cm x 18 cm x 4 cm)

Yardage Requirements

Yardage is based on 43"/44"
(109 cm/112 cm) wide fabric.
  ¹/₄ yd (23 cm) of muslin fabric
    for redwork, redwork lining,
    and pincushion lining
  Scraps of assorted red print
    fabrics
You will also need:
  ¹/₂ yd (46 m) of HeatnBond®
    fusible fleece (20" [51 cm] wide)
  Red pearl cotton #8
  1 cup (240 ml) of fine sand

Cutting the Pieces

*Follow **Rotary Cutting**, page 88, to cut*
pieces. Square for redwork is cut larger
than needed and will be trimmed after
embroidering. All measurements include
¹/₄" *seam allowances.*

From muslin fabric:
- Cut 1 **square** 5¹/₂" x 5¹/₂".
- Cut 1 **square lining**
  5¹/₂" x 5¹/₂".
- Cut 2 **pincushion linings**
  7¹/₂" x 7¹/₂".

From assorted red print fabrics:
- Cut 1 **back** 7¹/₂" x 7¹/₂".
- Cut 1 **strip #1** 1¹/₂" x 3¹/₂".
- Cut 1 **strip #2** 1¹/₂" x 4¹/₂".
- Cut 1 **strip #3** 1¹/₂" x 4¹/₂".
- Cut 1 **strip #4** 1¹/₂" x 5¹/₂".
- Cut 1 **strip #5** 1¹/₂" x 5¹/₂".
- Cut 1 **strip #6** 1¹/₂" x 6¹/₂".
- Cut 1 **strip #7** 1¹/₂" x 6¹/₂".
- Cut 1 **strip #8** 1¹/₂" x 7¹/₂".

From fusible fleece:
- Cut 4 **fleece squares**
  7¹/₂" x 7¹/₂".

•PINCUSHION•

Making the Redwork Square

Use the bird and heart patterns, page 12, from
Around the Town quilt. Or you may choose to use
another small design from any of the other projects
that is smaller than 3" x 3". Embroidery stitches
shown on page 5.

1. Refer to photo and follow **Transferring the Design**, page 4, to transfer bird and heart patterns onto **square**.
2. Use **square lining** and refer to **Lining Your Fabric**, page 4, to line square.
3. Using red pearl cotton, Stem Stitch design.
4. Centering stitched design, trim square to 3¹/₂" x 3¹/₂".

Making the Pincushion

*Follow **Machine Piecing**, page 89, and **Pressing**, page 90, to make pincushion. Use 1/4" seam allowances throughout.*

1. Sew **Strip #1**, then **Strip #2** to **square** to make **Unit 1**.

Unit 1

2. Sew **Strip #3**, then **Strip #4** to **Unit 1** to make **Unit 2**.

Unit 2

3. Sew **Strip #5**, then **Strip #6** to **Unit 2** to make **Unit 3**.

Unit 3

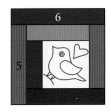

4. Sew **Strip #7**, then **Strip #8** to **Unit 3** to make **top**. Top should measure 7 1/2" x 7 1/2".

Top

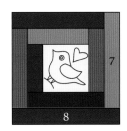

5. Following manufacturer's instructions, fuse 1 **fleece square** to wrong side of top. Fuse 1 fleece square to wrong side of **back**.

6. Matching right sides and leaving a 3" opening on 1 edge, sew top and back together. Turn right side out.

7. Fuse 1 fleece square to wrong side of each **pincushion lining**.

8. Matching *fleece sides*, using a short length stitch, and leaving a 3" opening on 1 edge, sew linings together. Turn so that fleece is facing out.

9. Pour sand into lining. Working stitches very close together, stitch opening closed.

10. Insert filled lining into top/bottom. Stitch opening closed.

Hexagon
TABLE·TOPPER

Finished Table Topper Size: 18" (46 cm) diameter

Yardage Requirements

Yardage is based on 43"/44" (109 cm/112 cm) wide fabric.

    7 scraps of assorted cream tone-on-tone print fabrics
      (each at least 7" x 7" [18 cm x 18 cm]) for hexagons
    20" x 20" (51 cm x 51 cm) **square** of red dot print fabric
    20" x 20" (51 cm x 51 cm) piece of fabric for **square lining**
    ³/₈ yd (34 cm) of fabric for binding
    23" x 23" (58 cm x 58 cm) piece of fabric for backing

You will also need:

    23" x 23" (58 cm x 58 cm) piece of batting
    Seven 3" (76 mm) purchased paper hexagon templates, *optional*
    Freezer paper
    Red pearl cotton #8

Making the Hexagon Center

1. If using purchased hexagon templates, skip to **Step 2**. To make hexagon template from freezer paper, trace hexagon pattern, page 87, onto dull side of freezer paper. Cut out template along traced line. Make 7 hexagon templates.

2. Center and pin 1 purchased template *or* center and press 1 freezer paper template (shiny side down) to wrong side of 1 cream fabric scrap. Cut fabric approximately $1/4$" outside template edges.

3. Fold and finger press 1 seam allowance over template. Working counterclockwise and mitering fabric at corner, fold adjacent seam allowance over template. Backstitch at mitered corner (**Fig. 1**) to hold fabric in place, stitching only through the fabric.

Fig. 1

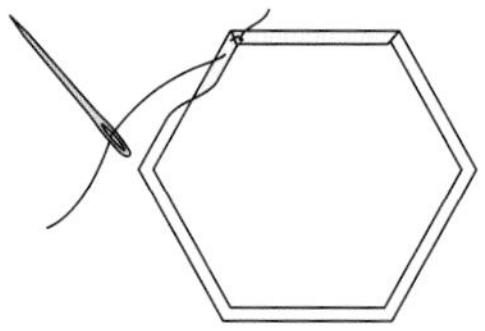

4. Use a long running stitch along side of hexagon to hold thread in place and backstitch at next corner. Continue to fold and stitch seam allowances, taking a backstitch at each corner to make **hexagon** (**Fig. 2**).

Fig. 2

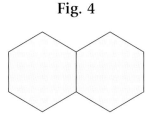

5. Repeat **Steps 2–4** to make a total of 7 hexagons.

6. Matching right sides and corners, place 2 hexagons together as shown in **Fig. 3**. Avoiding stitching through paper and backstitching at beginning and end of seam, whipstitch edges together along one side. Open pieces flat (**Fig. 4**).

Fig. 3

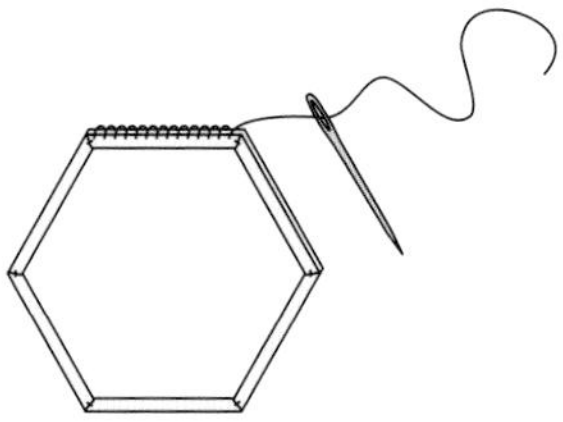

Fig. 4

7. Whipstitch 1 edge of each remaining hexagon to one of the hexagons in Step 6, opening pieces flat after adding each hexagon. Whipstitch each edge between hexagons, until **hexagon center** is completed.

Hexagon Center

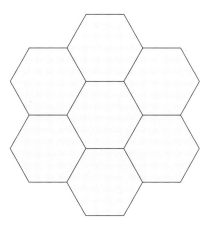

8. Carefully remove templates.

Appliquéing the Hexagon Center

1. Center and pin hexagon center to **square**; hand baste in place.
2. Use a sharps needle with a single strand of general-purpose sewing thread in color to match hexagon center; knot one end. Blindstitch (page 95) hexagon center to square.
3. Turn square over and use sharp scissors or specially designed appliqué scissors to trim away background fabric approximately ¹/₄" from stitching line. Take care not to cut appliqué fabric or stitches.

Adding the Redwork

Redwork patterns are on pages 86–87. Embroidery stitches are shown on page 5.

1. Refer to photo, page 83, and **Table Topper Diagram** and follow **Transferring the Design**, page 4, to transfer patterns onto hexagon center.
2. Use **square lining** and refer to **Lining Your Fabric**, page 4, to line square.
3. Using red pearl cotton, Stem Stitch design.

Trimming the Table Topper

1. Cut an 18" x 18" square of freezer paper. Fold paper in half vertically and horizontally.
2. For circle pattern, tie a length of string to a pencil. Insert thumbtack or pushpin in string 9" from pencil. Place thumbtack or pushpin at folded center of freezer paper. Holding string taut, draw a quarter circle (**Fig. 5**).

Fig. 5

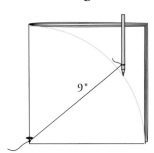

9"

3. Cut out freezer paper pattern along drawn line; unfold.
4. Centering freezer paper pattern over hexagon center, press pattern, shiny side down, to table topper top. Cut table topper top out along edge of pattern.

Completing the Table Topper

1. Follow **Quilting**, page 91, to mark, layer, and quilt as desired. Table topper shown was machine outline quilted ¹/₄" outside edge of hexagon center and ¹/₄" inside edge of center hexagon.
2. From fabric for binding, cut a 70" length of 2¹/₄"w bias strip, pieced as necessary. Matching wrong sides, press strip in half lengthwise to make binding. Follow **Attaching Binding**, **Steps 1** and **6–15**, page 93, to bind table topper.

Table Topper Diagram

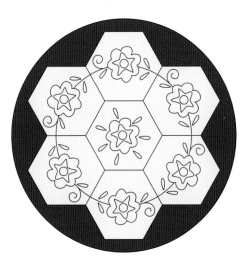

*Grey dashed line is for placement.
Do not transfer.*

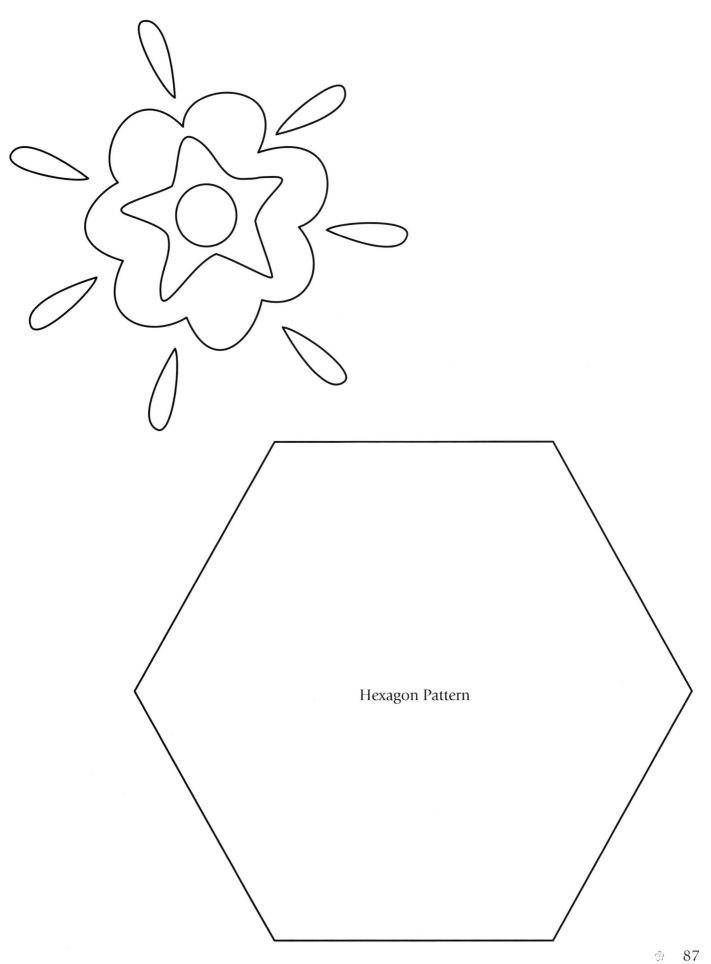

Hexagon Pattern

General INSTRUCTIONS

To make your quilting easier and more enjoyable, we encourage you to carefully read all of the general instructions, study the color photographs, and familiarize yourself with the individual project instructions before beginning a project.

Fabrics

SELECTING FABRICS
Choose high-quality, medium-weight 100% cotton fabrics. All-cotton fabrics hold a crease better, fray less, and are easier to quilt than cotton/polyester blends.

Yardage requirements listed for each project are based on 43"/44" wide fabric with a "usable" width of 40" after shrinkage and trimming selvages. Actual usable width will probably vary slightly from fabric to fabric. Our recommended yardage lengths should be adequate for occasional re-squaring of fabric when many cuts are required.

PREPARING FABRICS
We recommend that all fabrics be washed, dried, and pressed before cutting. If fabrics are not pre-washed, washing the finished quilt will cause shrinkage and give it a more "antiqued" look and feel. Bright and dark colors, which may run, should always be washed before cutting. After washing and drying fabric, fold lengthwise with wrong sides together and matching selvages.

Rotary Cutting
Rotary cutting has brought speed and accuracy to quiltmaking by allowing quilters to easily cut strips of fabric and then cut those strips into smaller pieces.

- Place fabric on work surface with fold closest to you.
- Cut all strips from the selvage-to-selvage width of the fabric unless otherwise indicated in project instructions.
- Square left edge of fabric using rotary cutter and rulers (**Figs. 1–2**).

Fig. 1

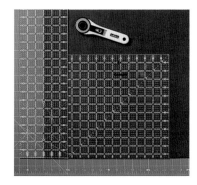

Fig. 2

- To cut each strip required for a project, place ruler over cut edge of fabric, aligning desired marking on ruler with cut edge; make cut (**Fig. 3**).

Fig. 3

- When cutting several strips from a single piece of fabric, it is important to make sure that cuts remain at a perfect right angle to the fold; square fabric as needed.

Machine Piecing

Precise cutting, followed by accurate piecing, will ensure that all pieces of project fit together well.

- Set sewing machine stitch length for approximately 11 stitches per inch.
- Use neutral-colored general-purpose sewing thread (not quilting thread) in needle and in bobbin.
- An accurate $1/4$" seam allowance is *essential*. Presser feet that are $1/4$" wide are available for most sewing machines.
- When piecing, always place pieces right sides together and match raw edges; pin if necessary.
- Chain piecing saves time and will usually result in more accurate piecing.
- Trim away points of seam allowances that extend beyond edges of sewn pieces.

SEWING STRIP SETS

When there are several strips to assemble into a strip set, first sew strips together into pairs, then sew pairs together to form strip set. To help avoid distortion, sew seams in opposite directions (**Fig. 4**).

Fig.4

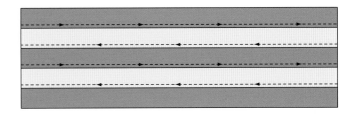

SEWING ACROSS SEAM INTERSECTIONS

When sewing across intersection of two seams, place pieces right sides together and match seams exactly, making sure seam allowances are pressed in opposite directions (**Fig. 5**).

Fig. 5

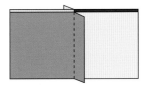

SEWING SHARP POINTS

To ensure sharp points when joining triangular or diagonal pieces, stitch across the center of the "X" (shown in pink) formed on wrong side by previous seams (**Fig. 6**).

Fig. 6

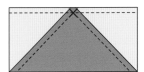

Pressing

- Use steam iron set on "Cotton" for all pressing.
- Press after sewing each seam.
- Seam allowances are almost always pressed to one side, usually toward darker fabric. However, to reduce bulk it may occasionally be necessary to press seam allowances toward the lighter fabric or even to press them open.
- To prevent dark fabric seam allowance from showing through light fabric, trim darker seam allowance slightly narrower than lighter seam allowance.
- To press long seams, such as those in long strip sets, without curving or other distortion, lay strips across width of the ironing board.

Machine Blanket Stitch

Some sewing machines feature a Blanket Stitch similar to the one used in this book. Refer to your owner's manual for machine set-up. If your machine does not have this stitch, try a zigzag stitch or any of the decorative stitches your machine has until you are satisfied with the look.

1. Thread sewing machine and bobbin with 100% cotton general-purpose sewing thread in desired weight.
2. Attach an open-toe presser foot. Select far right needle position and needle down (if your machine has these features).
3. Bring bobbin thread to the top of the fabric by lowering then raising the needle, bringing up the bobbin thread loop. Pull the loop all the way to the surface.
4. Begin by stitching 5 or 6 stitches in place (drop feed dogs or set stitch length at 0), or use your machine's lock stitch feature, if equipped, to anchor thread. Return setting to selected Blanket Stitch.
5. Most of the Blanket Stitch should be done on the piece being attached, such as a pocket, with the right edges of the stitch falling at the very outside edge of the piece. Stitch the edges indicated in project instructions.

6. *(Note: Dots on Figs. 7–8 indicate where to leave needle in fabric when pivoting.)* For outside corners (**Fig. 7**), stitch to corner, stopping with needle in background fabric. Raise presser foot. Pivot project, lower presser foot, and take an angled stitch. Raise presser foot. Pivot project, lower presser foot and stitch adjacent side.

Fig. 7

7. When stitching outside curves (**Fig. 8**), stop with needle down in background fabric. Raise presser foot and pivot project as needed. Lower presser foot and continue stitching, pivoting as often as necessary to follow curve.

Fig. 8

8. When stopping stitching, use a lock stitch to sew 5 or 6 stitches in place or use a needle to pull threads to wrong side of background fabric (**Fig. 9**); knot, then trim ends.

Fig. 9

Quilting

Quilting holds the three layers (top, batting, and backing) of the quilt together. Because marking, layering, and quilting are interrelated and may be done in different orders depending on circumstances, please read entire **Quilting** *section, pages 91–92, before beginning project.*

QUILTING A REDWORK QUILT

Redwork quilts often have very light quilting. And if the redwork pieces are small, they may not have any quilting at all. But larger redwork areas do require quilting or tacking. These areas and the rest of the quilt need to be quilted with an appealing look and the quilting should be evenly balanced.

One quilting option is free-motion quilting, treating the redwork like appliqués. You should add enough quilting to give definition and texture to the redwork fabric without adding so much detail that it detracts from the redwork.

Many antique redwork quilts were crosshatch quilted. Crosshatch quilting is done by quilting straight lines in a grid pattern. The lines may be stitched parallel to the edges of the quilt or stitched diagonally. This very traditional style of quilting can be stitched over the redwork. The thread should match the redwork fabric or you can use a clear, monofilament thread.

Using small French Knots or just tiny stitches to tack the redwork areas is another option. For smaller projects, quilting in the ditch might work well.

Or, you can simply frame your work without quilting it at all!

MARKING QUILTING LINES

Quilting lines may be marked using fabric marking pencils, chalk markers, or water- or air-soluble pens.

Simple quilting designs may be marked with chalk or chalk pencil after basting. A small area may be marked, then quilted, before moving to next area to be marked. Intricate designs should be marked before basting using a more durable marker.

Caution: Pressing may permanently set some marks. **Test** different markers **on scrap fabric** to find one that marks clearly and can be thoroughly removed.

PREPARING THE BACKING

To allow for slight shifting of quilt top during quilting, backing should be approximately 4" larger on all sides. Yardage requirements listed for quilt backings are calculated for 43"/44"w fabric. To piece a backing using 43"/44"w fabric, use the following instructions.

1. Measure length and width of quilt top; add 8" to each measurement.
2. Cut backing fabric into two lengths slightly longer than determined *length* measurement. Trim selvages. Place lengths with right sides facing and sew long edges together, forming tube (**Fig. 10**). Match seams and press along one fold (**Fig. 11**). Cut along pressed fold to form single piece (**Fig. 12**).

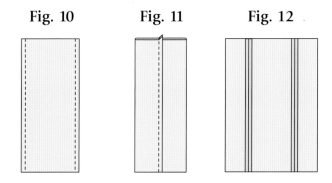

Fig. 10   **Fig. 11**   **Fig. 12**

3. Trim backing to size determined in Step 1; press seam allowances open.

CHOOSING THE BATTING

The appropriate batting will make quilting easier. For fine hand quilting, choose low-loft batting. All cotton or cotton/polyester blend battings work well for machine quilting because the cotton helps "grip" quilt layers. If quilt is to be tied, a high-loft batting, sometimes called extra-loft or fat batting, may be used to make quilt "fluffy."

Types of batting include cotton, polyester, wool, cotton/polyester blend, cotton/wool blend, and silk.

When selecting batting, refer to package labels for characteristics and care instructions. Cut batting same size as prepared backing.

ASSEMBLING THE QUILT

1. Examine wrong side of quilt top closely; trim any seam allowances and clip any threads that may show through front of the quilt. Press quilt top, being careful not to "set" any marked quilting lines.
2. Place backing *wrong* side up on flat surface. Use masking tape to tape edges of backing to surface. Place batting on top of backing fabric. Smooth batting gently, being careful not to stretch or tear. Center quilt top *right* side up on batting.
3. Use 1" rustproof safety pins to "pin-baste" all layers together, spacing pins approximately 4" apart. Begin at center and work toward outer edges to secure all layers. If possible, place pins away from areas that will be quilted, although pins may be removed as needed when quilting.

MACHINE QUILTING METHODS

Use general-purpose sewing thread in bobbin. Do not use quilting thread. Thread the needle of machine with general-purpose sewing thread or transparent monofilament thread to make quilting blend with quilt top fabrics. Use decorative thread, such as a metallic or contrasting-color general-purpose thread, to make quilting lines stand out more.

Straight-Line Quilting

The term "straight-line" is somewhat deceptive, since curves (especially gentle ones) as well as straight lines can be stitched with this technique.

1. Set stitch length for six to ten stitches per inch and attach walking foot to sewing machine.
2. Determine which section of quilt will have longest continuous quilting line, oftentimes area from center top to center bottom. Roll up and secure each edge of quilt to help reduce the bulk, keeping fabrics smooth. Smaller projects may not need to be rolled.
3. Begin stitching on longest quilting line, using very short stitches for the first $\frac{1}{4}$" to "lock" quilting. Stitch across project, using one hand on each side of walking foot to slightly spread fabric and to guide fabric through machine. Lock stitches at end of quilting line.
4. Continue machine quilting, stitching longer quilting lines first to stabilize quilt before moving on to other areas.

Free-Motion Quilting

Free-motion quilting may be free form or may follow a marked pattern.

1. Attach darning foot to sewing machine and lower or cover feed dogs.
2. Position quilt under darning foot; lower foot. Holding top thread, take a stitch and pull bobbin thread to top of quilt. To "lock" beginning of quilting line, hold top and bobbin threads while making three to five stitches in place.
3. Use one hand on each side of darning foot to slightly spread fabric and to move fabric through the machine. Even stitch length is achieved by using smooth, flowing hand motion and steady machine speed. Slow machine speed and fast hand movement will create long stitches. Fast machine speed and slow hand movement will create short stitches. Move quilt sideways, back and forth, in a circular motion, or in a random motion to create desired designs; do not rotate quilt. Lock stitches at end of each quilting line.

Making a Hanging Sleeve

Attaching a hanging sleeve to back of wall hanging or quilt before the binding is added allows project to be displayed on a wall.

1. Measure width of quilt top edge and subtract 1". Cut piece of fabric 7"w by determined measurement.
2. Press short edges of fabric piece 1/4" to wrong side; press edges 1/4" to wrong side again and machine stitch in place.
3. Matching wrong sides, fold piece in half lengthwise; sew long edges together.
4. Centering seam on back of hanging sleeve, press sleeve flat.
5. Center sleeve on back of quilt just below binding on top edge. Blindstitch top and bottom edges of hanging sleeve to backing, taking care not to stitch through to front of quilt.

Binding

MAKING SINGLE-FOLD STRAIGHT-GRAIN BINDING

1. With right sides together and using diagonal seams (**Fig. 13**), sew the short ends of the binding strips together to make one continuous strip for binding.

Fig. 13

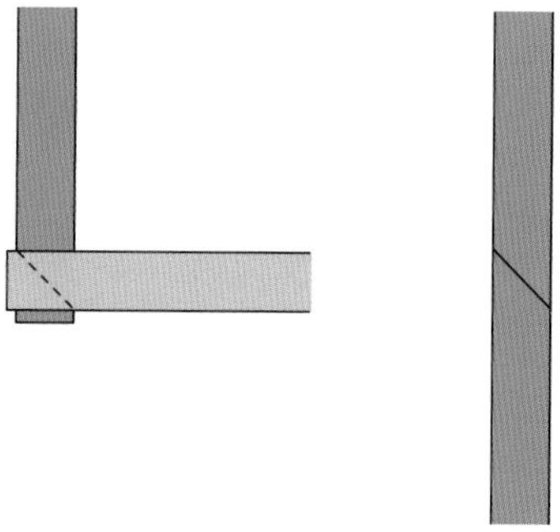

2. Trim seam allowances and press them open. Press one long edge of binding 1/4" to the wrong side.

MAKING DOUBLE-FOLD STRAIGHT-GRAIN BINDING

1. With right sides together and using diagonal seams (**Fig. 13**), sew the short ends of the binding strips together to make one continuous strip for binding.
2. Trim seam allowances and press them open. Matching wrong sides and raw edges, press strip in half lengthwise to complete binding.

ATTACHING BINDING

Instructions are written for binding a quilt with mitered corners, but the same technique may be used for binding other projects, such as the pillow sleeves or notions keeper.

Note: Figs. 14–25 show attaching double-fold binding. Single-fold binding is attached in the same manner, but will appear as shown in Fig. 14b.

1. Beginning with one end near center on bottom edge of quilt, lay binding around quilt to make sure that seams in binding will not end up at a corner. Adjust placement if necessary. Matching raw edges of binding to raw edge of quilt top, pin binding to right side of quilt along one edge.
2. When you reach first corner, mark 1/4" from corner of quilt top (**Figs. 14a–14b**).

Fig. 14a

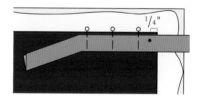

Fig. 14b

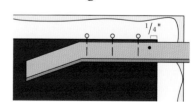

3. Beginning approximately 10" from end of binding and using ¹/₄" seam allowance, sew binding to quilt, backstitching at beginning of stitching and at mark (**Fig. 15**). Lift needle out of fabric and clip thread.

Fig. 15

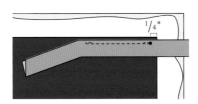

4. Fold binding as shown in **Figs. 16–17** and pin binding to adjacent side, matching raw edges. When you've reached the next corner, mark ¹/₄" from edge of quilt top.

Fig. 16   **Fig. 17**

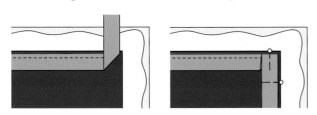

5. Backstitching at edge of quilt top, sew pinned binding to quilt (**Fig. 18**); backstitch at the next mark. Lift needle out of fabric and clip thread.

Fig. 18

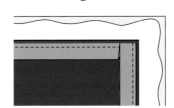

6. Continue sewing binding to quilt, stopping approximately 10" from starting point (**Fig. 19**).

Fig. 19

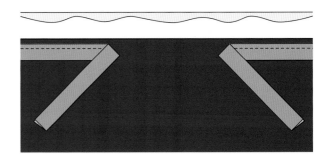

7. Bring beginning and end of binding to center of opening and fold each end back, leaving a ¹/₄" space between folds (**Fig. 20**). Finger press folds.

Fig. 20

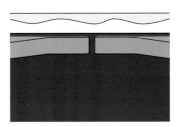

8. Unfold ends of binding and draw a line across wrong side in finger-pressed crease. Draw a line through the lengthwise pressed fold of binding at the same spot to create a cross mark. With edge of ruler at cross mark, line up 45° angle marking on ruler with one long side of binding. Draw a diagonal line from edge to edge. Repeat on remaining end, making sure that the two diagonal lines are angled the same way (**Fig. 21**).

Fig. 21

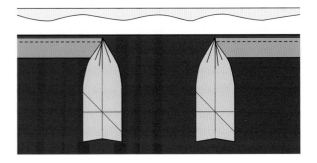

9. Matching right sides and diagonal lines, pin binding ends together at right angles (**Fig. 22**).

Fig. 22

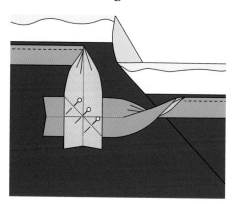

10. Machine stitch along diagonal line (**Fig. 23**), removing pins as you stitch.

Fig. 23

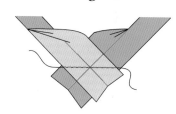

11. Lay binding against quilt to double check that it is correct length.
12. Trim binding ends, leaving ¹/₄" seam allowance; press seam open. Stitch binding to quilt.
13. Trim backing and batting even with edges of quilt top.
14. On one edge of quilt, fold binding over to quilt backing and pin pressed edge in place, covering stitching line (**Fig. 24**). On adjacent side, fold binding over, forming a mitered corner (**Fig. 25**). Repeat to pin remainder of binding in place.

Fig. 24   **Fig. 25**

15. Blindstitch binding to backing, taking care not to stitch through to front of quilt.

BLIND STITCH
Come up at 1, go down at 2, and come up at 3 (**Fig. 26**). Length of stitches may be varied as desired.

Fig. 26

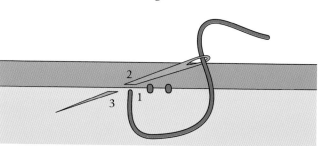

PAT'S MACHINE-SEWN BINDING
*For a quick and easy finish when attaching binding, Pat sews her binding to the **back** of the quilt and Machine Blanket Stitches or Straight Stitches it in place on the front, eliminating all hand stitching.*

1. Using a narrow zigzag, stitch around quilt close to the raw edges (**Fig. 27**). Trim backing and batting even with edges of quilt top.

Fig. 27

2. Beginning with one end near center on bottom edge of quilt, lay binding around quilt to make sure that seams in binding will not end up at a corner. Adjust placement if necessary. Matching raw edges of binding to raw edge of quilt top, pin binding to the **backing side** of quilt along one edge.

3. Follow **Steps 2–12** and **14** of **Attaching Binding**, page 93, folding binding over to quilt front to Machine Blanket Stitch, page 90, or Topstitch binding close to pressed edge (**Fig. 28**).

Fig. 28

Signing and Dating Your Quilt

A completed quilt is a work of art and should be signed and dated. There are many different ways to do this and numerous books on the subject. The label should reflect the style of the quilt, the occasion or person for which it was made, and the quilter's own particular talents. Following are suggestions for recording the history of the quilt or adding a sentiment for future generations.

- Embroider quilter's name, date, and any additional information on quilt top or backing. Matching floss, such as cream floss on white border, will leave a subtle record. Bright or contrasting floss will make the information stand out.

- Make label from muslin and use permanent marker to write information. Use different colored permanent markers to make label more decorative. Stitch label to back of quilt.

- Use photo-transfer paper to add image to white or cream fabric label. Stitch label to back of quilt.

- Make a label by working a small redwork design on a piece of muslin or other light fabric used in quilt top. Add information with embroidery or permanent fabric pen.

Metric Conversion Chart	
Inches x 2.54 = centimeters (cm)	Yards x .9144 = meters (m)
Inches x 25.4 = millimeters (mm)	Yards x 91.44 = centimeters (cm)
Inches x .0254 = meters (m)	Centimeters x .3937 = inches (")
	Meters x 1.0936 = yards (yd)

Standard Equivalents					
1/8"	3.2 mm	0.32 cm	1/8 yard	11.43 cm	0.11 m
1/4"	6.35 mm	0.635 cm	1/4 yard	22.86 cm	0.23 m
3/8"	9.5 mm	0.95 cm	3/8 yard	34.29 cm	0.34 m
1/2"	12.7 mm	1.27 cm	1/2 yard	45.72 cm	0.46 m
5/8"	15.9 mm	1.59 cm	5/8 yard	57.15 cm	0.57 m
3/4"	19.1 mm	1.91 cm	3/4 yard	68.58 cm	0.69 m
7/8"	22.2 mm	2.22 cm	7/8 yard	80 cm	0.8 m
1"	25.4 mm	2.54 cm	1 yard	91.44 cm	0.91 m

Inside Stories

Book 5

Study Guides for Children's Literature - Grades 7-8

Written by **Janice Montgomery** and **Candace Taff Carr**

Illustrated by **Jean Thornley**

Edited by **Dianne Draze** and **Sandy Woolley**

ISBN 931724-53-8